POP CULTURE-INSPIRED PROGRAMS
for Tweens, Teens, and Adults

POP
CULTURE-INSPIRED
PROGRAMS
for TWEENS, TEENS, *and* ADULTS

AMY J. ALESSIO | KATIE LaMANTIA | EMILY VINCI

ALA
Editions

CHICAGO | 2018

Extensive effort has gone into ensuring the reliability of the information in this book; however, the publisher makes no warranty, express or implied, with respect to the material contained herein.

ISBN: 978-0-8389-1705-3 (paper)

Library of Congress Cataloging-in-Publication Data

Names: Alessio, Amy J., author. | LaMantia, Katie, author. | Vinci, Emily, 1988- author.
Title: Pop culture-inspired programs for tweens, teens, and adults / Amy J. Alessio, Katie LaMantia, Emily Vinci.
Description: Chicago : ALA Editions, an imprint of the American Library Association, 2018.
Identifiers: LCCN 2018003535 | ISBN 9780838917053 (print : alk. paper)
Subjects: LCSH: Libraries—Activity programs--United States. | Young adults' libraries—Activity programs—United States. | Libraries—Special collections—Popular culture. | Popular culture—United States—History—20th century.
Classification: LCC Z716.33 .A438 2018 | DDC 027.62/6--dc23 LC record available at https://lccn.loc.gov/2018003535

Book design by Alejandra Diaz in the Charis SIL, Filson Soft and Alpha Echo typefaces.

♾ This paper meets the requirements of ANSI/NISO Z39.48–1992 (Permanence of Paper).

Printed in the United States of America
22 21 20 19 18   5 4 3 2 1

*Dedicated to my family as always.
Also for Katie and Emily, who inspire me and make me feel relevant
even though only one of us was alive in the '70s and '80s.*

....

*For all the Wonder Women in my life, but especially Amy and Emily.
And Alex—our story is just beginning.*

....

*To Amy and Katie, for their endless support and encouragement,
and my family, for keeping my feet on the ground but never trying
to take my head out of the clouds.
And to Kit, because our spin-off series lasted longer
than the original. ily.*

CONTENTS

Acknowledgments ***xi***
Introduction ***xiii***

1950s	**1**
Chex Mix and More: Nifty Fifties' Snacks	2
Everything Barbie	4
I Love Lucy	6
The Name Is Bond, James Bond	8
Make Your Own BBQ	11
Model Train Mania	13
'50s Chic: Poodle Totes	15
1960s	**17**
100 Years of Life: Board Game History and Challenges	18
Decoupage Daydream	20
Everything Denim	23
Holy Primetime, Batman! Superheroes on TV	26
Love Beads	28
Not Your Mother's Book Club: Books That Shocked	30
1970s	**33**
100 Years of RC and Model Airplanes	34
Domino Day	36

Erector Set, Tinkertoy, and Lincoln Log Challenges **39**

DIY Lava Lamps and Pet Rocks **41**

McDonald's Happy Meal Toys **43**

Retro Crafts: Pom-Poms, Macramé, Flower Looms, and More **45**

Tie-Dye **48**

Y.A., Why Not? The Golden Age of Young Adult Literature **50**

1980s   53

'80s Accessories **54**

Attack of the Brat Pack **57**

Ghostbusted **59**

Graffiti Art **62**

I Want My MTV **65**

Microwave Mania **68**

Pac-Man Party **70**

Rubik's Cube Challenge **74**

Strawberry Shortcake, Cabbage Patch Kids, ... **76**
and Other Hot '80s Toys

1990s   79

'90s Technology and Game Night **80**

Flair Fun **82**

Flannel Pillows **84**

Nickelodeon Nostalgia Night **86**

Pop Music: Boy Bands and Girl Power! **91**

Riot Grrrl Celebration: Zine and Button Making **94**

2000s 97

Cake Pops 98

Collector Con 100

Cult Movie Fest 102

Marvel Madness 104

Reality TV in Real Life 107

Revenge of the Nerds 110

TR-Not-So-L 114

Pop Culture Review 117

Classic Candies by the Decade 118

Classic Cars 120

Decades of Disney 122

Fashion Trendsetters 126

Games 129

Popular Franchises 132

Reboot Month 136

Treats and Beats by the Decade 138

About the Authors **141**
Index **143**

ACKNOWLEDGMENTS

Special thanks to Jamie Santoro for her continued support and to the staff at ALA Editions for their amazing work, and to the patrons of the Schaumburg Township District Library for their enthusiasm and participation.

INTRODUCTION

Pop culture—it's all around us. From the shows we watch to the clothes we wear, the music we listen to, and the games we play, even where we eat and spend our free time, popular culture infuses our daily lives for better or worse. Though the pervasiveness of cultural trends and the ease with which we access them have grown exponentially since the advent of communication media such as cable television and, especially, the Internet, previous decades were not without their own trends and cultural touchstones. If anything, pop culture has proven to be somewhat cyclical, as trends from the 1980s, eventually considered passé as the decade gave way to the '90s, reemerged in the early part of the 2000s as once again fashionable.

As we continually strive for fresh and relevant programming to keep our patrons engaged and interested, we often look to the future and the next big thing. We pick up on the newest and hottest trends and move on when something has lost its luster. However, the aforementioned cyclicity of pop culture as well as the current boom in nostalgia as trendy open the door to a wealth of programming in which the old is once again new. Here we lay out, decade by decade, programming ideas based on trends past and, in many cases, once again present.

HOW DO YOU LEARN TRENDS?

Pop culture trends can pop up overnight, while others can be predicted with more certainty. Nostalgia never goes out of style, and pop culture trends are often cyclical, with similar topics appearing every few years. Although trends can sometimes be elusive and difficult to predict, the following tips, tricks, and resources can help you navigate the waters of pop culture to create timely and relevant programming for your patrons.

- Seek out movie release dates for potential big-name movies. These movies may be a reboot of a classic film, a popular book to movie adaptation, or fandom based, or they might be generating a lot of chatter on the Internet.

- Are a lot of students or patrons talking about a specific topic? Do you consistently hear one TV show being discussed by teens? Have a conversation and find out more information.

- Look for trending topics on Twitter and check Google Analytics for searched keywords.

- Are there many memes about a specific topic or issue circulating on social media?

- Are multiple books (both fiction and nonfiction) being published about a particular topic? Seek out clues in book reviews and reading that would indicate that a particular setting, theme, subject, or time period has become popular across different books or genres.

- Have clothes and accessories that were popular in previous years suddenly come back into fashion with younger generations?

- Check the "Best Of" lists and forecasted trends that come out at the beginning of each year.

- Reach out to coworkers and have conversations about their pop culture interests to involve varying personalities, interests, and departments in your library programming.

The following resources can help you find and identify trends:

- *BuzzFeed*: Great for lists and nostalgia-based programming ideas

- *The A.V. Club*: Provides reviews and commentaries about new and upcoming pop culture media

- *Entertainment Weekly*: Helpful for movie and TV show releases and recaps

- *Tumblr*: Can keep you up to date on fandoms and great ideas on how to incorporate them into your library programs

PAST TRENDS THAT WILL WORK TODAY

Planning programs that appeal is never an exact science. There will always be inexplicable hits or misses with events. Building on current interests while keeping with popular culture is a challenge. In trying to determine which elements of popular past trends will be a hit with patrons now, keep some of the following considerations in mind.

- **Does it make sense in today's world?** Jiffy Pop Stove-Top Popcorn was very appealing, but people are not cooking it over their stoves anymore because there are easier and faster alternatives.

- **Is the type of program appealing?** If craft programs are a hit with the seniors or teens in your community, then those same crafters will likely want to try the themed versions described in this guide. If programs about fashion or board games do not appeal in your area, these versions may bring in new folks but will perhaps not be as popular as the ones that already build on community interests. If you aren't sure what types of programs have the most appeal, offer a survey to learn what people will most likely attend by themselves or with their families.

- **What types of patrons are coming in?** What ages of patrons dominate which programs? Are the family crafternoons packed but the millennials events are just growing? Analyzing attendance will help with strategizing library events.

- **What do your circulation figures show?** Those stats are not just for weeding! Use them to see what interests your patrons. How often and how recently have the value guides for collectors of toys or ephemera gone out? Which titles are stolen? Which books on what events in recent history are most popular?

- **Are there tie-ins with recent pop culture hits?** *Stranger Things* happened, and libraries built displays with holiday lights and alphabet letters. Because the show was set in the 1980s, interest in that program might lead to interest in other '80s programs. Although program planning in libraries sometimes happens months in advance, the prevalence of sequels gives a chance to offer relevant popular programs when those sequels are released.

- **Are there elements of past trends that can be updated?** No one wants to make macramé plant hangers anymore, but program participants may like mini terrariums or macramé bookmarks. They may enjoy an element of popular past trends, applied in a new way. Although few are poaching eggs in the microwave as ads from the 1980s suggested, many would be interested in easy microwave meals for one or healthy microwave snacks. It may be easier to approach this question from the reverse—which popular trends have an element of past fads? STEM started with kits like Erector Sets and Tinkertoys. When past elements are brought back, older patrons will also enjoy the event. They may not build a Tinkertoy robot or team up with a group for building challenges, but they will enjoy a fun trip to their past adventures as they experience presentations or attend with their families.

BEST PRACTICES

1. Check your library's movie license agreements and the production companies for the movies you will be viewing before presenting them for the public or for a program.

2. There was no PG-13 rating for movies before 1984, and those films may have harsher language and more violence than your library may find acceptable.

3. Consider community partnerships in the area and explore how you can have a mutually beneficial relationship for a single program or for multiple programs. Such relationships can include promotion for a program, prizes, hosting an off-site program, new instructor opportunities, and more.

4. Be mindful of anniversaries, release dates, and revamps of pop culture entities that will affect your programming and give it a timely boost.

5. Cultural and societal norms have changed throughout the decades and have been captured forever in media. Be aware of content and stereotypes before showing movies and promoting books.

6. Be cognizant of cultural sensitivities associated or potentially associated with the subject matter of some of the programs listed in this guide.

7. If you are serving food or drinks at a program or if they are part of a program activity, make sure you have a list of ingredients available. Many patrons have food allergies and may not be able to take part in that specific activity.

8. Riskier programs that take place outdoors or involve physical activity may need to be approved of by management before you begin planning. Consider a waiver for a program involving risk to limit liability.

9. Communication is always important when planning programs. If you're planning a library-wide event, make sure management is on board and desk staff are informed about events and times.

10. Staff from all different areas of the library have varying interests and talents. Ask them for their opinions on pop culture programming. If they are interested in helping with planning a pop culture program, let them assist you, with the permission of their manager.

11. Nostalgia is a powerful factor and can be used as a theme and to promote your programs. Don't discount its value when planning for programs.

12. A lot of the programs in this book have appeal for patrons of all ages—including those younger than the youngest group covered here: tweens. Consider how you can make a program work to be inclusive of all your library patrons, both in and outside your specialty area.

HOW TO USE THIS GUIDE

The ideas for each topic are broken down into manageable portions. Enough ideas are listed under each program theme so that libraries may choose ones that work best in different communities. Many activities can be adapted to other themes and programs. Each program will have the following headings where appropriate:

- **Prep Time:** This section includes planning and shopping as well as setup time.

- **Length of Program:** This time is a suggestion for a stand-alone event, but more time may be needed to include all activities.

- **Number of Patrons:** This is a suggestion for the maximum number of people attending to make the activities most enjoyable. For example, craft programs should have fewer people if instruction and help will likely be needed.

- **Suggested Age Range:** This book offers programming suggestions for tweens (ages 10–13), teens (14–19), millennials (20–39), and older adults (40+), although other age ranges may be included now and then. Unless specified, if a program is recommended for millennials, it is not necessarily appropriate for all adults. Millennials like to engage with people who have similar frames of reference for popular culture, just as older adults do. The age ranges are suggested for optimal success of events. Some programs are appropriate for families to enjoy together, and those are specified.

- **Supplies/Shopping:** This section lists the items needed for the event. Activities and variations may require additional materials.

- **Activities:** This section explains how to run the program and includes some setup tips and ideas for experiences to include in programs.

- **Crafts:** These activities are designed for the suggested age range.

- **Trivia and Other Free Games:** These are easy ways to engage participants in the topic or to build interest before the event.

- **Marketing:** This section includes techniques and tips for displays and other advertising for each event.

- **Variations by Age Groups:** Ideas for adapting similar programs for different groups will be found here. Is there an aspect of this theme that tweens in particular may enjoy? If there is a way to add something to the event to make it more enjoyable for different age groups, that will be found here also.

- **Pro Tips:** These are specific or unusual ideas to enhance and simplify events.

1950s

S oda fountains, rock 'n' roll, and bobby-soxers were only part of the fun of the 1950s. The seven programs in this chapter are designed to bring the cuisine, dolls, fashions, and shows of the 1950s into today's world. "Chex Mix and More: Nifty Fifties' Snacks" will leave patrons with recipes and histories of some favorite snacks. "Everything Barbie" will appeal to collectors of all ages. "I Love Lucy" will bring those fans together again at the library. James Bond will *Live and Let Die* with his own themed event. DIYers will be surprised by how easy it is to "Make Your Own BBQ"—for indoors or outside. "Model Train Mania" will encourage patrons to make tracks to build their own system for the library. The "'50s Chic: Poodle Totes" program will inspire modern designers to reboot famous '50s designs. Patrons may find it hard to return to this century after rediscovering some past passions from the '50s.

CHEX MIX AND MORE: NIFTY FIFTIES' SNACKS

This event is fun to have during Super Bowl season, for men and women. Revisit past popular and easy snacks.

PREP TIME	LENGTH OF PROGRAM	NUMBER OF PATRONS	SUGGESTED AGE RANGE
2 hours	1½ hours	25–30	Millennials, older adults

SUPPLIES/SHOPPING

- Napkins
- Paper plates

Chex Mix (several varieties for participants to taste)
- Bowls, spoons for serving

BBQ Sauce
- Crockpot
- Large spoon
- Frozen meatballs
- Grape jelly (18 oz. jar)
- Chili sauce—any kind (18 oz. jar)

Bacon/PB Rollups
- Bacon, cooked (microwaved is fine)
- Peanut butter
- Toothpicks
- Knives

Cheez Whiz Chic
- Several cans of Cheez Whiz
- Several flavors of Ritz or other sturdy crackers

Mini Pizzas (optional)
- Toaster oven (at least a few)
- English muffins
- Shredded mozzarella
- Pizza sauce
- Olives
- Sliced pepperoni
- Canned mushrooms

ACTIVITIES

Set up stations for making each snack, with seats for eating.

- *Chex Mix*: Provide slips of paper next to bowls for people to vote on their favorite flavor.

- *BBQ Sauce*: Mix the chili sauce and grape jelly in the crockpot one hour before the program and put in the frozen meatballs on high (turkey or beef is fine).

- *Cheez Whiz Chic*: Invite participants to make elegant decorations on crackers with the aerosol cheese or simply enjoy the different flavors.

- *Bacon/PB Rollups*: An hour before the program, microwave strips of bacon. Participants will add peanut butter to the bacon strips, roll them up, and fasten them with toothpicks.

- *Mini Pizzas*: If toaster ovens are available, participants can make several English muffin pizzas at a time. Participants can add toppings and cook.

MARKETING

Make a display of football and Super Bowl party materials. Nearby, place recipes for Chex Mix with information about the program printed on the back.

VARIATIONS BY AGE GROUPS

- *Teens*: Have teens taste purchased snack mixes, such as Chex Mix and crackers, and vote on their favorites. Use aerosol Cheez Whiz sparingly!

- *Millennials*: Invite participants to bring in copies of favorite appetizer recipes to exchange. Host this event the afternoon before the Super Bowl as a pre-party and decorate purchased brownies in team colors.

EVERYTHING BARBIE

Though admittedly a polarizing figure, Barbie has been a pop culture icon in her own right since her debut in 1959. A program focusing on Barbie will appeal to patrons both young and old and provides a variety of programming options.

PREP TIME	LENGTH OF PROGRAM	NUMBER OF PATRONS	SUGGESTED AGE RANGE
4–5 hours	1 hour	25	Millennials, older adults

SUPPLIES/SHOPPING

Origami Dresses
- Origami paper in various colors and patterns

ACTIVITIES

- Bring in a presenter to talk about the history and cultural influence of Barbie. Consider reaching out to local antiques and collectibles shops and colleges or universities to find presenters. You can also do some research and see if there are Barbie collectors in your area who would be interested in speaking to the group.

- This program lends itself well to a crossover with the "Collector Con" program detailed in the "2000s" chapter of this book. If someone participating in the Collector Con is a collector of Barbies, consider asking that person to present a preview of the collection as a lead-up program to the Con.

- *Book Discussion*: Plenty has been written about Barbie and her cultural influence, so consider incorporating a book discussion into your programming plan. The following are some title suggestions:

  » Gerber, R. (2010). *Barbie and Ruth: The Story of the World's Most Famous Doll and the Woman Who Created Her*. New York: Harper.
  » Lord, M. G. (2004). *Forever Barbie: The Unauthorized Biography of a Real Doll*. Fredericton, NB: Goose Lane Editions.
  » Stone, T. L. (2010). *The Good, the Bad, and the Barbie: A Doll's History and Her Impact on Us*. New York: Viking.

CRAFTS

Origami Dresses
- Barbie is known for nothing if not fashion, so have patrons try their hand at creating some origami dresses using instructions that can be found easily online (for example, https://www.pinterest.com/explore/origami-dress/).

TRIVIA AND OTHER FREE GAMES

Barbie has been a part of our cultural consciousness for more than fifty years, and in that time she's racked up plenty of factoids and anecdotes that make perfect trivia questions!

MARKETING

Chances are your library's children's department contains various Barbie books and DVDs, so use those, as well as any books about Barbie that the reference department has, to create a display. If you are able to, include some Barbies in the display, too. An additional option is to ask your coworkers if they have any pictures from their own childhoods or their children's or grandchildren's childhoods that show them playing with Barbies and create a collage to feature on the display. Include on the display information about the program.

VARIATIONS BY AGE GROUPS

Tweens, teens: Design your own Barbie. Part of the controversy surrounding Barbie is her representation of unrealistic body expectations. Although in recent years there has been a concerted effort to create dolls with differing body types and representing various career choices, some would say there is still work to be done. Invite your tween and teen patrons of all genders to create their own Barbie by drawing or collaging the aspects and characteristics they would like to see represented. In addition to markers, crayons, and paper, provide old magazines that participants can cut up to create their vision. Remember, it's not an art contest, it's an opportunity for expression.

I LOVE LUCY

Thanks to the magic of syndication, *I Love Lucy* is still enjoyed regularly by audiences today. Although younger audiences are perhaps less interested in the show than their older relatives are, that doesn't mean they can't participate in and enjoy a program celebrating this iconic show, its star, and the 1950s.

PREP TIME	LENGTH OF PROGRAM	NUMBER OF PATRONS	SUGGESTED AGE RANGE
3–4 hours	1 hour	25	Millennials, older adults

SUPPLIES/SHOPPING

Chocolate Tasting
- Assorted chocolates (be as fancy—or not—as you want!)
- Plates
- Napkins
- Vinyl checkerboard tablecloths

Origami Dresses and Coats
- Origami paper in various colors and patterns (especially damask)

Checkers
- Checkers, checkerboards

ACTIVITIES

- *Chocolate Tasting*: Spread out that checkerboard tablecloth and invite your patrons to sample various delicious chocolates (no need to go Lucy-and-Ethel-style).

- *Makeup and Hair Tutorial*: If it's within your budget, consider hiring an expert (or perhaps you have one on staff!) who can lead a tutorial or demonstration about that classic 1950s look. Check with local beauty salons and schools for leads on experts in your area.

- *'50s Playlist*: Be sure to have a playlist featuring the hits of the '50s to set the mood!

CRAFTS

Origami Dresses and Coats

- There is no doubt that Lucille Ball wore some seriously gorgeous dresses and coats on the show—even if we only got to see them in black and white. Patrons can have fun creating their own beautiful dresses and coats using instructions that can be found easily online (for example, https://www.pinterest.com/explore/origami-dress/).

TRIVIA AND OTHER FREE GAMES

- *1950s Trivia*: Whether it's classic TV, the trends, the fashions, the events of the decade, or a little bit of everything, there's a wealth of material to create a 1950s trivia throwdown.

- *Checkers*: You've got the tablecloths, why not go all in and set out some checkerboards, too?

MARKETING

Create a display of DVDs and books that feature *I Love Lucy* and other TV shows of the 1950s. Add some CDs with the greatest hits of the '50s, too, and include information on the display about the program.

VARIATIONS BY AGE GROUPS

Tweens, teens: Because tweens and teens will not likely be very interested in *I Love Lucy*, focus on the time period for a program that's geared toward these patrons. Blow patrons' minds by creating a sock hop program complete with a root beer float station, a photo booth with '50s props, and *Grease* karaoke. Young patrons might also enjoy the vintage makeup and hair tutorials.

THE NAME IS BOND, JAMES BOND

Ian Fleming's James Bond novels have withstood the test of time since debuting in 1953. The book and movie franchises have spurred a decades-long affair with audiences that remains relevant even as new 007s have come and gone. Spies, gadgets, and the allure of the dangerous and mysterious Bond are still just as exciting today.

PREP TIME	LENGTH OF PROGRAM	NUMBER OF PATRONS	SUGGESTED AGE RANGE
2 hours	1 hour	20–40	Older adults

SUPPLIES/SHOPPING

Martini Mixology
- Martini glasses
- Garnishes (lemon slices, olives)
- Vodka
- Martini mixer or cocktail shaker
- Ice cubes
- Vermouth
- Gordon's Gin
- Kina Lillet
- Champagne glasses

Book Discussion
- James Bond novels
- British snacks (scones, Turkish Delight, etc.)
- Tea
- Cups
- Napkins

Keep Talking and Nobody Explodes
- Computer or game system

Escape Room
- Breakout EDU
- Pencils
- Paper

ACTIVITIES

- *Martini Mixology*: Learn how to make James Bond's specialty drink: a martini, shaken, not stirred. Mix things up by trying the Vesper, which Bond orders in *Casino Royale* ("Three measures of Gordon's, one of vodka, half a measure of Kina Lillet. Shake it very well until it's ice-cold, then add a large thin slice of lemon peel."). This program would require the library to have a liquor license for the day. Alternatively, you could create mocktails or virgin martinis.

- *Book Discussion*: Create a special book club event themed around the James Bond novels. Read one of the original Ian Fleming novels, such as *Casino Royale*, and one of the newer books by the ghostwriters and discuss how they compare. Serve tea and British snacks such as scones and Turkish Delight.

- Invite a local professor or guest lecturer to explain the differences among intelligence agencies across the world, particularly the British Secret Intelligence Service, or MI6. Invite your patrons to learn about the differences between the British secret service and ambassadors and about how the intelligence agencies and spies operate in the world today.

- *Keep Talking and Nobody Explodes*: Test your James Bond bomb defusing skills with the game Keep Talking and Nobody Explodes. One player is trapped in a virtual room with a ticking time bomb that the player must defuse while the other players, without seeing the bomb, give the instructions for defusing the bomb using the expert guidance found in the bomb defusing manual. The game can be played on a computer or video game system (a variety of platforms are available) for a one-time, low cost with new scenarios and bomb defusings each time.

- *Escape Room*: Create an escape room designed around spies, codes, ciphers, and James Bond. Use Breakout EDU (https://www.breakoutedu.com/digital/) or create your own game using numerous online tools such as the Khan Academy (https://www.khanacademy.org/computing/computer-science/cryptography#concept-intro) or Rumkin (http://rumkin.com/tools/cipher/).

TRIVIA AND OTHER FREE GAMES

- Create a list of Bond villains and Bond girls and see if your participants know which ones are real or fake. Have participants create their own Bond villain name!

- List all the actors who have played James Bond and the movies since the '50s. Participants must match the Bond to the movie, and the one with the most correct Bonds wins.

MARKETING

- Create a scavenger hunt in your library or a fiction display themed around James Bond. Ask your patrons to find key Bond items, such as a bow tie, a magnifying glass, a classic Matchbox car, a globe, and more. Provide pens, pencils, and paper or use geocaches to amp up your patrons' scavenger hunt skills. At key points, don't forget to advertise your Bond program!

- Create a display and ask your patrons to vote for their favorite Bond actor or Bond villain.

VARIATIONS BY AGE GROUPS

- *Tweens, teens*: Create your own spy training obstacle course. This activity is inexpensive and can be done using in-house equipment and materials. Have participants crawl under chairs or tables, maneuver through tight spaces, and practice their balance. To amp up your obstacle course, borrow cones and balance blocks from your youth services department.

- *Tween, teens*: Bring in a karate instructor to teach basic self-defense maneuvers to your tween and teen patrons. Although they may not look as cool or practiced as James Bond, participants can learn the beginnings of his training and find out how he got out of some sticky situations. Participants might develop a serious interest in martial arts and a good general knowledge of self-defense.

- *Tweens, teens*: These age groups will also love escape rooms themed around spies. Create or choose codes or ciphers that they can work together to decode. If they are interested in learning more about the life of a spy, direct them to the CIA website to gather more intel.

> **PRO TIP**
>
> **This program has** great potential crossover with "Classic Cars" and "Popular Franchises" in the "Pop Culture Review" chapter for Bond-themed nights and vice versa.

MAKE YOUR OWN BBQ

Backyard BBQs were fashionable in the 1950s and are still a hit. Many vintage cookbooks feature ways to create your own grill for cooking. Offer this fun program on how to construct your own BBQ, or make it part of a weekly series of backyard delights featuring a chef showing unusual foods for the grill and another showing indoor grilling. This event could even be part of a garden series with programs on patio and garden design. This description will feature options for creating a mini grill.

PREP TIME	LENGTH OF PROGRAM	NUMBER OF PATRONS	SUGGESTED AGE RANGE
2 hours	45 minutes for each type of grill	25	Millennials, older adults

SUPPLIES/SHOPPING

Choose one type of grill to make if desired.

Tin Can Grill (prior to the program, ask staff members to donate large tin cans for the event)
- Tin cans (large number 10 size)
- Several sets of tin snips
- Heavy-duty foil
- Small grilling racks

Mini Planter Tabletop Grill
- Mini terra-cotta planters
- Mini adjustable cake pans (2 per grill)
- Wire mesh
- Metal glue
- Wire cutters
- Drill with bit

Flowerpot Hibachi
- 10-inch terra-cotta planters
- Pot saucers (2 per planter; one will go underneath, and one will extinguish flames after cooking)
- Sand
- Foil
- Small grilling racks

ACTIVITIES

- Show photos of wheelbarrow grills, wagon grills, beach cooking, and more as the participants arrive. An inexpensive option for this program is to demonstrate different ways to make grills, hand out supply lists, and let participants make their own grills at home.

  Note: If you have made samples of the indoor grills and are in a well-ventilated area, you could provide shish kebabs for patrons. This may also be a good outdoor event.

- *Tin Can Grill*: See Dian Thomas's blog (www.dianthomas.com/a-improvised grills.htm) for instructions on making this outdoor grill. Using the tin snips, foil, and racks, participants will easily be able to make this grill.

- *Mini Planter Tabletop Grill*: The blog *A Subtle Revelry* (http://asubtlerevelry .com/table-top-grill/) has easy instructions for making these indoor grills. Participants will put together a mini terra-cotta planter with wire mesh inside and mini cake pans.

- *Flowerpot Hibachi*: See The Spruce.com (https://www.thespruce.com/how -to-make-a-flower-pot-grill-334985) for easy directions for making an indoor 10-inch terra-cotta hibachi.

TRIVIA AND OTHER FREE GAMES

True or False Ingredients: Invite players to choose which of a list of unusual ingredients could be used in BBQ sauce, pulling from online resources or cookbooks.

MARKETING

Hand out recipes for easy BBQ sauces or cooking with information about the program on the back.

VARIATIONS BY AGE GROUPS

- *Teens*: Invite teens for an after-hours outdoor cooking event in the parking lot of the library. Provide basic skewer foods such as cubed meats, cheeses, and vegetables for teens to roast in addition to s'mores fixings. Mini burgers and hot dogs could also work. Music and dancing can be included, or you can provide an outdoor screen and a movie for a longer event.

- *Millennials, older adults*: If the library is surrounded by houses with yards and patios, invite a speaker from a home building store to show options for putting together a brick grill or oven.

MODEL TRAIN MANIA

By the end of the 1950s, model trains were giving way to space toys, but there was still plenty of interest in Lionel and Thomas toy trains. The National Toy Train Museum has wonderful videos and information that may be useful in planning a program for toy train enthusiasts (http://nttmuseum.org/library/index.shtml). The National Model Railroad Association is another good source (https://www.nmra.org/).

PREP TIME	LENGTH OF PROGRAM	NUMBER OF PATRONS	SUGGESTED AGE RANGE
2 hours	2 hours	25 for some activities, drop-in for playing with trains	Older adults, families

SUPPLIES/SHOPPING ·······································

Bulletin Board (covered; tracks may be drawn on)
- Colored paper for making train cars
- Markers

Decorating Library Tracks
- Set of wooden train track pieces (available as a building set online at Amazon and other retailers)
- A few wooden Thomas trains
- Sharpies or glow-in-the-dark paint to decorate track
- Brightly colored paints
- Paintbrushes

Train Painting
- Wooden train cars to paint
- Paints
- Paintbrushes

Candy Trains
- Hot glue guns (for adults to use) and glue sticks
- Peppermints
- Packs of gum
- Rolos
- Life Savers rolls
- Wrapped Hershey's Kisses
- Small wrapped Hershey bars

ACTIVITIES

- *Bulletin Board*: In the month prior to the program, have paper available so people can cut out and decorate their own paper train cars. Make a large bulletin board for people to attach their train cars to, as an advertisement for the program.

- *Decorating Library Tracks*: Invite families to decorate a piece of track at a maker station in the month before the program. They can paint it, add their names, and decorate with paint or markers. (Choose a theme, such as glow in the dark, bright colors, or rainbow.) You can either have families sign up for a fifteen-minute slot of time to do this or set it up as a drop-in station. These tracks will be used for the program and later in the library. The maker station will need paint, brushes, and water. Each family can get a piece of track when they sign in or at the desk when they drop in.

- Invite a local model train group to set up a small display or demonstration for the event, either prior to or on the day of the program.

- Also, set up a table for the painted tracks to be arranged and played with during the event.

- *Candy Trains*: Instructions for making candy trains can be found at Mavis Butterfield's blog *One Hundred Dollars a Month* (https://www.onehundred dollarsamonth.com/how-to-make-a-candy-train-easy-kids-christmas-crafts/). A section for the candy train making should be placed near outlets for the glue guns. A staff member should stay at that station to help adults with the gluing.

- *Train Painting*: Set up a painting station for the wooden toy train cars, with brushes and water. These cars may be taken home.

MARKETING

The bulletin board and track painting activity will help advertise this event.

VARIATIONS BY AGE GROUPS

Older adults: If there is interest, invite model train group members to speak about collecting trains and about trends. The event may garner more interest around holiday times when a train could be set up as a decoration in a part of the library that adults frequent.

'50S CHIC: POODLE TOTES

No other garment says 1950s like poodle skirts. The whimsical skirt was designed by Juli Lynne Charlot in 1947 when she added holiday appliqués to a circle skirt she made out of felt. She designed several types of appliqués for the skirts as people bought them from her, and eventually the popular poodle became a favorite. This program revisits '50s designs with information on how to make easy appliqués to decorate a tote bag and how to wear scarves '50s style.

PREP TIME	LENGTH OF PROGRAM	NUMBER OF PATRONS	SUGGESTED AGE RANGE
2 hours (more to make samples)	1½ hours	25	Older adults

SUPPLIES/SHOPPING

- Tote bags
- Several colors of felt squares
- Fabric glue
- Needles and thread
- Fabric scissors
- Ribbons (several bargain spools, no wider than ½ inch)
- Glue-on gems and embellishments
- Pom-poms (assorted colors)
- Googly eyes
- Fusible web material—4 yards for 25 appliqués
- Irons
- Ironing boards
- Markers and Sharpies
- Paper
- Pencils
- Nylon fashion scarves (optional)

ACTIVITIES

- Play 1950s music in the room to set the mood. Set up stations for cutting, ironing, and gluing. Display photos of 1950s fashions, especially poodle skirts.

- Everyone can design an appliqué of a pet or hobby and draw the design on paper before cutting the pieces from felt. If someone is designing a poodle, for example, she will draw and cut the poodle outline on felt.

- Appliqués can be glued on to the tote bags or fused with fusible web. Hand sewing can also be done with needles and thread. Once the appliqués are fused or sewn on, they can be decorated with pom-poms, Sharpies, and other embellishments, using the fabric glue.

- Those who desire can glue on ribbon "leashes" from the appliqué to the edge of the tote.

- While projects are drying or people are waiting for the iron, demonstrate '50s scarf chic—neck, purses, hair—and let people experiment with theirs.

MARKETING

At prior programs with seniors or other adults, wear a scarf or show a sample tote and discuss the event.

VARIATIONS BY AGE GROUPS

- *Tweens*: Prior to Halloween, help tweens make their own No-Sew Circle Skirts. An easy pattern can be found on the *ObSEUSSed* blog (www.obseussed .com/2011/05/make-no-sew-poodle-skirt.html). Tweens can also make poodles and glue them on, along with "leashes."

- *Millennials*: This age group may enjoy learning some '50s dance moves or watching some popular 1950s movies along with making the appliqué totes and tying the scarves.

1960s

Make love, not war with programs inspired by the 1960s. Patrons will celebrate "100 Years of Life" with board game challenges and fun for different ages. "Decoupage Daydream" will help patrons easily create lovely items while enjoying themselves. Jeans, purses, and more return in an interactive "Everything Denim" program that makes everything old new again. "Holy Primetime, Batman! Superheroes on TV" celebrates Bruce Wayne and his alter ego so fans of all ages will see different eras. Who doesn't love beads? "Love Beads" 2010s-style adds strings of fun at this interactive event. And wrap up the 1960s with a visit to Peyton Place and other memorable destinations with "Not Your Mother's Book Club: Books That Shocked."

100 YEARS OF LIFE: BOARD GAME HISTORY AND CHALLENGES

Tween and teens are thinking about life choices. Invite them for an afternoon of board gaming and challenges.

PREP TIME	LENGTH OF PROGRAM	NUMBER OF PATRONS	SUGGESTED AGE RANGE
2 hours	2½–3 hours with crafts	25	Tweens, teens

SUPPLIES/SHOPPING

- 4 versions of Life board game
- Snacks (optional)

Life Tile and People Keychains
- Spare Life tiles, people, and cars
- Keychain hardware
- Pliers
- Jump rings (at least ½-inch)
- Hole punch
- Wire cutters
- Hot glue gun, glue sticks

DIY Board Games
- Markers
- Scissors
- Glue
- Buttons
- Mini plastic toy cars
- Dice
- Card stock (for tiles, cards)

ACTIVITIES

- *Game Challenges*: Everyone should be able to free play the game for at least fifteen minutes when they arrive. Then challenge participants at each table to play for ten minutes before switching to the next table and continuing that game. The boards stay on the tables, the games continue—but the people move. All players end up at their original board—to see what changed. Other challenges include letting no one choose college, looking at winning dollar amounts, and having a contest to see who ends up with the most children or finishes the fastest.

- *Variation*: Another way to run this event is to provide unusual versions of Life (including Star Wars) and invite groups to play. The blog *Brilliant Maps* lists several versions (http://brilliantmaps.com/game-of-life/).

- *DIY Board Games*: Several websites have printable board games, including this LoveToKnow page (http://boardgames.lovetoknow.com/Create_Your_Own _Printable_Board_Game). Invite teens or teams to design their own board games. See if any group wants to design a fandom version, such as a Shadowhunters Life. When participants finish, make the games available for other teens to play and use in the teen area.

- *Life Flash Fiction*: Give audience members ten minutes to write a Life game flash fiction describing any aspect of the game.

CRAFTS

Life Tile and People Keychains
- Punch holes in the top of a Life tile. Using the tools, add jump rings and attach to the keychain hardware. Glue people and mini cars as desired.

TRIVIA AND OTHER FREE GAMES

Make an online quiz with Life game–type choices on Playbuzz.com and use on library social media to advertise the program.

MARKETING

In the teen area of the library, make "paths" from squares of paper with Life game choices and questions and include information about the program at the bottom of each square.

VARIATIONS BY AGE GROUPS

- *Families*: Offer a board game–playing afternoon just for fun. The printable DIY board games could also be made as a family craft.

- *Older adults*: Offer several different games popular in past decades for free play. If possible, invite a toy collector to discuss the value of collecting past board games.

DECOUPAGE DAYDREAM

Decoupage is a timeless craft that can be enjoyed by patrons of any age. It's a great opportunity to upcycle as well as get a little messy. Library patrons might be more familiar with the term *Mod Podge*, but you can give them a pop culture history lesson by showing them how folks crafted in the '60s—including making decoupage glue from scratch.

PREP TIME	LENGTH OF PROGRAM	NUMBER OF PATRONS	SUGGESTED AGE RANGE
1–2 hours	1 hour	20	Tweens, teens, millennials

SUPPLIES/SHOPPING

Decoupage Glue
- Water
- Flour
- Sugar
- Vegetable oil

Soup Can Succulent Holders, Pencils, Mason Jars
- Paintbrushes
- Foam brushes
- Scissors
- Rulers or tailor's measuring tapes
- Thin patterned paper, discarded newspapers and magazines, scrapbook paper, discarded or withdrawn library books
- Unsharpened number 2 pencils
- Small mason jars
- Empty, clean soup cans
- Tiny succulents
- Cactus or succulent soil

ACTIVITIES

Combine the following to make decoupage glue:
- 1 cup water
- 1½ cups flour
- ¼ cup sugar
- ¼ teaspoon vegetable oil

CRAFTS

Soup Can Succulent Holders

- STEP 1: Remove the labels from the soup cans, then wash and dry the cans.

- STEP 2: Decide if you want to cover the can with a solid piece of paper or with several smaller pieces. (*Note*: If you want to cover the can with one solid piece of paper, you will need to measure the can from top to bottom and around to know what size paper you will need. After measuring the can, cut a piece of paper to the correct size.)

- STEP 3: Paint a generous amount of Mod Podge or decoupage glue around the outside of the can.

- STEP 4: Adhere paper to the outside of the can.

- STEP 5: Paint Mod Podge or decoupage glue over the paper once you have all the paper in place.

- STEP 6: Let the glue dry. (Patrons may need to take the container home with them to allow the glue to dry completely, in which case you'll want to have small containers for transporting the soil and succulents for replanting at home.)

- STEP 7: Add the cactus or succulent soil and the succulents.

Pencils

- STEP 1: Cut thin patterned paper into 6½-by-1½-inch strips.

- STEP 2: Brush a light layer of Mod Podge or decoupage glue onto the back of a strip of paper.

- STEP 3: Wrap the strip of paper around a pencil slowly, making sure to flatten out any air bubbles and wrinkles as you go.

- STEP 4: Let dry completely.

Mason Jars

- STEP 1: Paint a generous amount of Mod Podge or decoupage glue around the outside of the jar.

- STEP 2: Add bits of paper to the outside of the jar.

- STEP 3: Paint Mod Podge or decoupage glue over the paper.

- STEP 4: Let dry completely.

MARKETING

Make some sample decoupage items and use them in a display along with any Mod Podge or decoupage craft books that your library has. Include information about the program on the display.

VARIATIONS BY AGE GROUPS

The variations here involve simply changing up the items that are being decoupaged at the program. Ideally you want to feature items that will be useful to those participating, which will be different. Other items that are easy to decoupage are picture frames (wooden), wine bottles, notebooks, and coasters.

EVERYTHING DENIM

Denim burst onto the fashion scene in the '60s and '70s and quickly became part of mainstream clothing. Many pop culture iconic moments are associated with denim, from James Dean and Marlon Brando in *Rebel Without a Cause* to the counterculture movement in the '60s to bell-bottoms. There are multiple ways to upcycle and use old pieces of jeans as part of your programming. If you plan multiple programs, you can practically use the whole pair of jeans!

PREP TIME	LENGTH OF PROGRAM	NUMBER OF PATRONS	SUGGESTED AGE RANGE
4 hours	1½ hours	15	Tweens

SUPPLIES/SHOPPING

Denim Bags and Purses
- Jean shorts or pants
- Embellishments (colorful or patterned fabric, decorative patches, ribbons, etc.)
- Sewing needles
- Thread
- Scissors
- Tacky glue
- Ruler

Denim Board
- Jean pockets
- Scissors
- Foam core
- Tacky glue or hot glue gun and glue sticks
- Embellishments

Denim Journal Cover
- Jeans
- Scissors
- Hot glue gun and glue sticks
- Embellishments
- Puff paints or Sharpies
- Choice of material to cover (journal, diary, e-reader, book, etc.)

Denim Bracelets

- Jean seams
- Scissors
- Snap fasteners
- Hot glue gun and glue sticks
- Scraps of fabric and stones (lace, buttons, gems, etc.)

CRAFTS ··

Denim Bags and Purses

- Put tattered jeans to good use and upcycle them into colorful denim purses. Take a pair of jean shorts (or jeans cut to shorts length) and cut the legs off evenly across. Turn the fabric inside out and cut open the crotch fabric at the seam along with any excess material in the middle. Sew across the bottom (and bring the material down from the middle) to close up the gaps and form the base of your new purse or bag. Use pant materials or additional fabric to make the straps.

    If you have sewing machines, this is an excellent time to use them, but the project can also be done easily by hand sewing. If there's time or extra materials, patrons can add embellishments such as patches or ribbons or even add an interior fabric lining to their bag.

Denim Board

- Jean pockets can be used to organize a tween's messy life. Tweens can customize their own foam core boards with colorful embellishments or personal pictures and use back jean pockets to store school supplies, pictures, jewelry, tchotchkes, hairbrushes and accessories, and more. Collect jeans from staff or scavenge thrift stores in advance of the program. Have participants cut out the back pockets of each pair of jeans, including the exterior denim. Tweens can choose how many pockets they want to use and organize them on their boards. Patrons then glue the interior of the back pocket to the foam core board while leaving the nice denim exterior open to contain items.

Denim Journal Covers

- Create a journal cover using pieces of denim from a pair of jeans. Cut a patch from a pair of jeans that is large enough to cover both the front and back covers of the journal, with at least an extra inch of material on all sides. If you can, cut a patch that has a pocket on it (front or back) to create a pencil holder. With the journal open, line up the material on all sides and glue to the front and back covers. Once dry, repeat the process with the material inside the covers and cut off the excess material. Once dry, add fun decorations such as flowers or ribbons to the outside covers. Use puff paint or Sharpies for lettering. This project can also be modified for book, diary, or even e-reader covers.

Denim Bracelets

- Cut the seams from denim pants, shirts, or shorts to form cuffs or bracelets. For instructions, see the blog *Dragonflys and Stars* (https://dragonflysandstars .blogspot.com/2012/03/scrappy-denim-bracelets.html). Make sure the band fits around the patron's wrist and has a little overlap where the fasteners will snap together. Use hot glue to connect the points of the fastener to the bracelet, one on the top of the fabric and the joining piece on the opposite side of the fabric on the bottom. Alternatively, crafters can use a button and create a hole in the fabric on the opposite end to secure it. Tweens can decorate their bracelets at will with the embellishments your library provides. This is a great chance to clean out your closet, and it is a cheap program to do on the fly. Tech up this program by using wearable electronics in your denim bracelet program (https://www.slideshare.net/alitseng/wearable-electronics-1).

MARKETING

- Create a sample of one of the projects and use it at a service desk at your library. Store materials or put flyers advertising the program in the denim pockets.

- Promote the program with a flyer and advertise it in the crafts section in the nonfiction collection. If you have a picture of one of the crafts, be sure to include it.

VARIATIONS BY AGE GROUPS

- *Millennials, older adults*: Create decorative and handy wine bags or carriers out of jean pants. Cut the pant leg below the knee (skinny jeans are easiest), flip the material inside out, and sew up or hot glue the bottom. Turn the material right side out and decorate at will. Participants just tie a ribbon around the neck of the bottle when they use it or give it away.

PRO TIP

Provide a standard empty wine bottle for patrons to experiment with and determine what size to make their carriers.

- *Millennials, older adults*: Many of the projects in this program can be adapted for millennials and older adults. Denim purses and denim bags can be made to hold laptops and tablets. The denim foam core board can be used to organize mail and bills, holiday greeting cards, or children's school information.

PRO TIP

Jeans and denim are easy to find in secondhand stores when gathering your materials. To do these programs on even more of a shoestring budget, ask staff or patrons to donate jeans or ask participants to bring along a pair of jeans when they attend the program.

HOLY PRIMETIME, BATMAN! SUPERHEROES ON TV

Sure, superheroes are everywhere you look today—in countless TV shows, movies, and video games—but there was once a time when superheroes were not nearly as ubiquitous in pop culture. A handful of superheroes graced the small screen during the golden age of TV, and a program highlighting the humble live-action origins of these heroes is sure to draw patrons old and young alike.

PREP TIME	LENGTH OF PROGRAM	NUMBER OF PATRONS	SUGGESTED AGE RANGE
3–4 hours	1–1½ hours	25	Older adults

SUPPLIES/SHOPPING

- Baking sheets (inexpensive at thrift stores)
- Spray adhesive
- Decorative fabric
- Scissors

ACTIVITIES

- If you're able to, show episodes or clips from classic superhero TV series like *The Incredible Hulk, Batman,* and *Wonder Woman,* as well as others.

- If you're close to a college or university, look into finding someone who is knowledgeable about television history or the history of superheroes in media to do a presentation.

- Consider adding elements of the "Chex Mix and More" program in the "1950s" chapter to give attendees a tasty treat to eat!

CRAFTS

DIY TV Trays

- The age of superheroes on TV was also the dawn of the age of TV dinners. Play on that theme by including a craft that shows fun ways to upcycle old baking sheets into new-looking serving trays.

» STEP 1: Cut a piece of fabric big enough to cover the front of the tray and wrap around to the back.

» STEP 2: Spray the front of the tray with spray adhesive and lay the fabric down over it.

» STEP 3: Smooth the fabric down, being sure to get rid of any air bubbles. Continue to smooth over the edges of the tray.

» STEP 4: Flip the tray over and cut a piece of fabric big enough to cover the part that is still exposed.

» STEP 5: Spray the back of the tray with adhesive and attach the fabric.

TRIVIA AND OTHER FREE GAMES

- A plethora of trivia exists about any of the television series that featured superheroes. You can also, of course, expand to asking questions about the superheroes featured in general.

- *Guess the Superhero*: Describe the hero and have people guess the name. Include Batman, Wonder Woman, Electra Woman and Dyna Girl, Isis, the Incredible Hulk, the Green Hornet, the Bionic Woman, Shazam, Superman, and Spider-Man.

MARKETING

Create a display of DVDs that feature classic superhero television series, as well as volumes of the current DC Batman '66 and Wonder Woman '77 comics, and include on the display information about the program.

VARIATIONS BY AGE GROUPS

Tweens, teens, millennials: DC Comics now has two series that feature the superheroes as they appeared in each of their television shows: Batman '66 and Wonder Woman '77. Consider having a book discussion on one volume of these series and pairing it with a viewing of an episode (or more than one) of the shows. Another option is to view a current superhero film (such as one of the Tim Burton or Christopher Nolan Batman movies or the 2017 Wonder Woman movie) and pairing it with the television series featuring the same hero, discussing the differences and the different goals the movies and TV shows are trying to achieve.

LOVE BEADS

This simple craft is a great addition to any program, but it also stands well on its own as a relaxed drop-in. Younger patrons may be well acquainted with making friendship bracelets but are perhaps less familiar with this vintage craft.

PREP TIME	LENGTH OF PROGRAM	NUMBER OF PATRONS	SUGGESTED AGE RANGE
2 hours	1–2 hours (depending)	20–25	Tweens, teens

SUPPLIES/SHOPPING

- Nylon beading string (.38 mm or thinner)
- Beads in assorted colors (Try to stick with natural beads, like stones, wood, and seed beads. Although crystals are beautiful, they may be too sparkly for a hippie-inspired look.)
- Scissors
- Strong glue
- Coloring pages (optional)
- Colored pencils, crayons, markers (optional)

ACTIVITIES

As mentioned, this is a fun and low-key program. Once your materials are set out for patrons, turn on a 1960s playlist and let the groovy times (and, we hope, not any stray beads) roll! The following instructions are from "Crafts of the '60s" (https://hubpages.com/games-hobbies/60sCrafts):

- STEP 1: Measure out and cut a length of nylon bead string. Love beads are generally long, so the necklace should at least hit the bottom of your rib cage. Tie a knot on one end of the string, leaving about 3 inches of string at both ends.

- STEP 2: Bead your necklace. String the beads randomly or create a pattern.

- STEP 3: Leave about 3 inches of string unbeaded. Tie a knot on the end of the string, ending the necklace. Double-knot the ends together. Snip off the excess string and gently tuck the ends into a bead on each side. Place a drop of strong glue on the knot and allow it to dry fully.

CRafts ·

Coloring Pages

- If you'd like to provide an additional craft, consider setting out 1960s-inspired coloring pages. A Pinterest search for "coloring pages 1960s free printable" yields a lot of results for free pages.

MaRKETING ·

Create a photo display of fashions from the '60s (focusing primarily on love beads, of course), and include on it books, movies, and CDs that have particularly '60s-esque covers. Also include, of course, information about the program.

VaRIATIONS BY aGE GROUPS ·

Variations aren't necessary for this program. It's great for all ages and makes an especially good intergenerational program for parents to do with their younger children.

NOT YOUR MOTHER'S BOOK CLUB: BOOKS THAT SHOCKED

Before *Fifty Shades* brought new erotica readers into the library, *Peyton Place* shocked readers everywhere. Would you like to shake up your book club? Consider a live or online Book Shock Club.

PREP TIME	LENGTH OF PROGRAM	NUMBER OF PATRONS	SUGGESTED AGE RANGE
1½ hours	1 hour per book, plus time for viewing shows or movies	22	Millennials, older adults

SUPPLIES/SHOPPING

- Copies of the book to be discussed, if possible
- Copy of the television show or movie of each title
- Snacks, drinks (optional)

ACTIVITIES

- For each book discussion, give a brief overview of the date of publication, the reaction to the book, and any relevant information about the author.

- The following questions apply to all the books:

  » What was the most surprising moment?
  » Has this book held up and, if not, what elements are dated?
  » Was there a segment of the population that was particularly shocked by this book?
  » Is there a recent book that is similar?
  » Is this a good quality book? Why or why not?
  » Why was this book popular?
  » Did any character have an arc? Please describe.

- Invite each participant to submit a question on a card and draw randomly to discuss until time is up.

- Show the movie or TV show, or at least the ending. Ask the group to compare the book to the film or program.

- The following are possible titles to discuss and view:

  » *Peyton Place* by Grace Metalious
  » *The Thorn Birds* by Colleen McCullough
  » *Forever . . .* by Judy Blume (see also "Y.A., Why Not?" in the "1970s" chapter)
  » *The Stepford Wives* by Ira Levin
  » *Rosemary's Baby* by Ira Levin
  » *Valley of the Dolls* by Jacqueline Susann
  » *The Da Vinci Code* by Dan Brown
  » *Fifty Shades* Trilogy by E. L. James
  » *Push* by Sapphire
  » *The Lovely Bones* by Alice Sebold

MARKETING

Bright signage and images of the covers will let people know what the discussions are about.

VARIATIONS

Online: This book club could "meet" online to discuss the titles and reconvene after people watch the media. The club could have a Yahoo! group, a Facebook page, or a real-time Google Hangout.

1970s

With bell-bottoms, mustaches, and disco, the 1970s had memorable styles. But there was a lot more to these ten years, and some of it transfers well to activities for today's patrons. In "100 Years of RC and Model Airplanes," patrons of all ages will learn about and make airplanes. The history of model aircraft from the 1870s through drones will be featured. "Domino Day" will offer people of all ages an opportunity to play the game or set up unique courses to knock down. There are even edible dominoes to enjoy! Before STEM there were Erector Sets, Tinkertoys, and Lincoln Logs. The program described in this chapter offers building fun with those classic toys. Memorable 1970s fads included lava lamps and pet rocks, and new ways to make these items are described in the "DIY Lava Lamps and Pet Rocks" program. Collectors will appreciate the fun "McDonald's Happy Meal Toys" event highlighting some of the best meal toys. Patrons will enjoy a crafting time warp when they remake some "Retro Crafts," from pom-poms to woven barrettes. Crafts from the past wouldn't be complete without "Tie-Dye." Wrapping up the 1970s programs is "Y.A., Why Not? The Golden Age of Young Adult Literature," which delves into the works of S. E. Hinton, Judy Blume, and other unforgettable authors.

100 YEARS OF RC AND MODEL AIRPLANES

Nikola Tesla patented the first version of radio control (RC) in 1898, and the first airplane models utilizing it appeared in the 1930s. The first RC airplane contest was in 1937, but RC clubs were still popular in the 1970s and beyond. The rise of the drone is refueling interest in RC aircraft. Participants in this program will make simple RC model airplanes and learn more about where they can fly them recreationally.

For more information, visit the following websites:

- *Academy of Model Aeronautics*: www.modelaircraft.org/museum/radiocontrol .aspx
- *R/C Airplane World* (links to clubs): https://www.rc-airplane-world.com/rc-air plane-clubs.html

PREP TIME	LENGTH OF PROGRAM	NUMBER OF PATRONS	SUGGESTED AGE RANGE
1 hour	1½ hours	25	Families

SUPPLIES/SHOPPING

- Drinking straws
- Card stock
- Elmer's glue—sticks and liquid
- Markers
- Scissors
- Origami paper
- RC airplane kits (optional; available on Amazon or other places for a range of prices)

ACTIVITIES

- Invite an RC aircraft hobbyist to talk to the group for fifteen to twenty minutes and show some planes. People from local clubs may be able to talk about the hobby and ways to get involved.

- Discuss drones and where they can be flown in the area.

- Seat the participants in groups at tables. Allow twenty-five to thirty minutes for patrons to build an airplane with the straws, card stock, and paper. Let the planes dry.

- While the planes are drying, everyone can make a paper airplane. It may be helpful to have books or instructions available on how to fold them. Participants can take turns flying their creations in a designated corner of the room.

- When the models are dry, participants may try to fly them and adjust the designs if needed.

- *Optional*: Provide four remote control airplane kits for groups to build and try at this event.

- *Optional*: Have a few RC small aircraft for families to take turns flying.

MARKETING

- Two weeks prior to the event, put up a display of patrons' models. Offer awards for the oldest model, the smallest model, and the largest model (if there is a secure way to display it).

- Hang some model airplanes from the ceiling around the library to help advertise the event. Information about the program could hang from the planes on small signs.

VARIATIONS BY AGE GROUPS

Tweens: *Drone Photo Contest*—After the holidays, when some younger people may have received drones as gifts, schedule a time when drones can fly around outside the library building taking photos. Then post the photos on social media. If possible, consider allowing an after-hours drone photo time inside the library, too.

DOMINO DAY

Domino Day refers to an event set up to break the world record in toppling dominoes. Host a different type of Domino Day at your library with these fun events, including game instruction, mini toppling challenges, and more. Domino shows with fancy chain reactions became popular in the 1970s, so this program would tie in well with decade or anniversary events, or simply present it as a fun gaming day.

PREP TIME	LENGTH OF PROGRAM	NUMBER OF PATRONS	SUGGESTED AGE RANGE
1½ hours	3 hours	50	Tweens, teens, older adults, families

SUPPLIES/SHOPPING

Several sets of dominoes from thrift stores or purchased inexpensively in bulk (many unmarked dominoes for toppling and races can be bought in lots)

Domino Brownies
- Brownies
- White frosting
- Black gel pens
- Chocolate chips
- Small paper plates
- Plastic knives
- Napkins or paper towels

Make a Domino Set
- Several 12-inch felt squares
- Sharpies
- Fabric scissors
- Rulers
- Pens

Domino Magnets
- Magnet sheets (with adhesive side)
- Dominoes

ACTIVITIES ···

- *Toppling Competition*: Set up a space for domino toppling. Allow free play or set times for mini challenges. Challenges could involve small teams, each using the same number of dominoes and making chains of standing dominoes that stretch from one area to another (before being knocked down) or that go over a stack of books or that are set up within a time limit.

- *Races*: Each team of two will set up the same number of dominoes in the same area for races to see which setup will topple first.

- *Four-Player Games*: Set up tables with instructions for traditional domino games or variations.

- *Solitaire*: Have instructions for patrons to learn how to play solitaire domino games as a handout to take home, or demonstrate.

- *Tournament*: Set up hourly tournaments with the first twelve to sixteen people who come to play, or in pairs, with winners playing each other until one remains. The traditional score of 250 points could be lowered for the tournament to 100, or each table could have a time limit. The player with the highest number of points at the end of play is the winner.

- *Domino Brownies*: Patrons can decorate brownies with frosting, gel, and chocolate chips to resemble dominoes.

CRAFTS ··

Make a Domino Set
- Participants should measure and mark their felt squares into 2-by-1-inch rectangles before cutting. Fabric scissors are sharp, so this activity should have a staff member nearby or be limited to people age 14 and up. After the felt is cut, people can decorate their sets with the Sharpies.

Domino Magnets
- Dominoes can be made into refrigerator magnet games or accessories. Before the program, cut the magnetic sheets into the shape of the dominoes. Patrons can adhere the magnetic sheets to dominoes and then use a few for a mini refrigerator game or make just one for a decoration.

MARKETING

Place domino games on tables in the public areas of the library to raise interest. Have information about the program on bookmarks that look like a domino on one side.

VARIATIONS BY AGE GROUPS

- *Millennials*: In addition to the toppling and game events, millennials may enjoy fortune telling. Domino fortune telling has a historical basis and may be fun. Place instructions with the codes on a table with a set of dominoes and let people try to tell their own fortune for fun. Possible layouts and codes can be found in many places online. One source is the "Advanced Gypsy Domino Fortune Telling" page of the Domino-Play website (www .domino-play.com/Games/FortuneGypsyAdvanced.htm).

- *Tweens*: In addition to the toppling, races, games, and crafts, tweens may enjoy learning some magic tricks with dominoes. The "Magic/Psychic Dominoes" page of the Domino-Play website has several magic tricks to learn with dominoes (www.domino-play.com/Magic.htm).

- *Older adults*: *Domino Club*—Offer tables and space with a few sets if older adults want to just come visit and play during a specified time each week in the library.

ERECTOR SET, TINKERTOY, AND LINCOLN LOG CHALLENGES

Building toy crazes from the '70s are the precursors of STEM events. Let families, tweens, or teens experience a nostalgic trip back with these free-form, team-building activities.

PREP TIME	LENGTH OF PROGRAM	NUMBER OF PATRONS	SUGGESTED AGE RANGE
1½ hours	1½ hours	20–25	Tweens, teens, families

SUPPLIES/SHOPPING

- Basic Erector Set (available from Amazon or Costco)
- Two large Lincoln Log sets
- Two large Tinkertoy sets

Edible Tinkertoys
- Small plates
- Marshmallows in different sizes
- Pretzels

ACTIVITIES

Set up five stations—one for the Erector Set and two each for the Tinkertoys and Lincoln Logs. Provide basic instructions for a few models at each station. Invite teams to move every fifteen minutes or so and build something different at each station.

CRAFTS

Edible Tinkertoys
- Provide small plates with a selection of pretzels and marshmallows so participants can make a person or a vehicle (and then eat it).

MARKETING

Have a drop-in play station for all ages near the checkout area with information about the program and some pieces from one of the sets.

VARIATIONS BY AGE GROUPS

Millennials: Provide several Lincoln Log or Tinkertoy sets and set up timed challenges for teams to make houses or vehicles.

> **PRO TIP**
>
> **To ensure that** no person is dominating a building group and that everyone is getting a turn making things, have a smaller group, provide more sets, or set up this program as a drop-in with a fifteen-minute limit at each station.

DIY LAVA LAMPS AND PET ROCKS

This easy program is great for a screen-free summer afternoon at the library. It's also an inadvertent reminder to today's tweens and teens to be extra thankful for that iPhone, because it could be just a rock.

PREP TIME	LENGTH OF PROGRAM	NUMBER OF PATRONS	SUGGESTED AGE RANGE
2–3 hours	1 hour	20	Tweens, teens

SUPPLIES/SHOPPING

Lava Lamps
- Water
- Alka Seltzer
- Food coloring
- Clear bottles (ideally ones that have a "decorative" look: Snapple bottles, fancy water bottles, etc.)

Pet Rocks
- Rocks (either fresh from outside or from a craft supply or outdoor store; ideally ones that have at least one flat, smooth surface)
- Acrylic paint
- Paintbrushes
- Sharpies

Optional Additional Supplies
- Hot glue gun and glue sticks
- Googly eyes
- Colorful yarn or pipe cleaners
- Glitter
- Buttons

ACTIVITIES

Lava Lamp (see http://on.mash.to/2ukaOxW)

- STEP 1: Mix 1 cup of water with the food coloring of your choice.

- STEP 2: Fill the bottle three-quarters full with water.

- STEP 3: Add the colored water to the bottle, making sure to leave about an inch from the top of the bottle.

- STEP 4: Break one Alka Seltzer tablet into small pieces.

- STEP 5: Add the pieces into the bottle one at a time, waiting a few seconds between each piece so that the bottle doesn't overflow with bubbles.

- STEP 6: Once all the pieces have been added, put the lid on the bottle and enjoy! Once the fizz has run out, the bottle will settle. To start it back up, just add Alka Seltzer!

Pet Rock

- Rinse the rocks well, especially if they've just come from outside. Make sure they are completely dry before participants start decorating.

- Once the rocks have been washed and dried, it's all up to the patrons!

MARKETING

Create a display of pet books from the fiction section and include books about geology and archaeology. Do the same thing with books about interior decorating and ones about volcanoes. With each display include a sign that asks, "Can you guess what we're talking about?" or a similar question to encourage your patrons to guess "pet rock" and "lava lamp." Include on the display information about the program.

VARIATIONS BY AGE GROUPS

Variations aren't necessary for this program. It's great for all ages and makes an especially good intergenerational program for parents to do with their younger children.

McDONALD'S HAPPY MEAL TOYS

No stranger to changing the world of food and how we consume it, McDonald's did it again in June 1979 with the introduction of the Happy Meal. The toy that was included with the kids' meal started out simple and has evolved into an entity that's desirable all on its own. Many people have collected Happy Meal toys over the years, and this program is a celebration for all ages.

PREP TIME	LENGTH OF PROGRAM	NUMBER OF PATRONS	SUGGESTED AGE RANGE
1–2 hours	1 hour	25	Millennials, older adults

SUPPLIES/SHOPPING

- Crayola air-dry clay (assorted colors; you can also use a polymer clay, but because it requires baking to set, it is slightly more cumbersome than air-dry clay)

- Popsicle sticks, toothpicks, and the like for shaping and adding details to the clay sculptures

ACTIVITIES

- If it's feasible for your library (and if such a person exists in your area), consider bringing in someone such as a historian to talk about the history of McDonald's and the Happy Meal toy. For a discussion focused more specifically on the Happy Meal toy, consider reaching out to local collectibles stores. If they don't have anyone on staff who can give a talk, perhaps they'll be able to put you in touch with someone who can. Another speaker option is someone from a collectibles store or comics shop who can talk about toy collecting in general and its relation to pop culture.

- This program lends itself well to a crossover with the "Collector Con" program detailed in the "2000s" section of this book. If someone participating in the Collector Con is a collector of Happy Meal toys, consider asking that person to give a talk or preview of the collection as a lead-up to the Con.

CRAFTS

DIY McDonald's Toys

- Set up a station at which attendees can make their own small toys out of Crayola air-dry clay. Because air-dry clay takes at least twenty-four hours to dry, patrons will not be able to paint it at the program, so provide different colors of the clay so that patrons can add colorful elements.

TRIVIA AND OTHER FREE GAMES

McDonald's Trivia: A simple Internet search for "McDonald's trivia questions and answers" yields many results, so you'll have no trouble putting together a McDonald's trivia contest.

MARKETING

Put together a display of books and documentaries about toy collecting featuring Happy Meal toys (if you have or can get some; *hint*: they are inexpensive at thrift stores), and include on the display information about the program.

VARIATIONS BY AGE GROUPS

No variations necessary—this program is great for all ages!

RETRO CRAFTS: POM-POMS, MACRAMÉ, FLOWER LOOMS, AND MORE

Many adults can remember making a macramé plant hanger or pom-poms for roller skates. Although this program offers time only to sample these retro crafting skills, a lot of interest may signal the need for another, follow-up program. For example, if many participants spend time at the quilling station, you could plan a more advanced quilling program.

PREP TIME	LENGTH OF PROGRAM	NUMBER OF PATRONS	SUGGESTED AGE RANGE
2 hours	1½ hours	25	Tweens, teens, millennials, older adults, families

SUPPLIES/SHOPPING

Pom-Poms
- Yarn
- Scissors
- Strips of cardboard (1½ inches wide by 4 inches long)

Macramé
- Clipboards (to hold the projects)
- DMC embroidery floss
- Safety pins

Ribbon Barrettes
- Metal barrettes with two parallel bars, or split barrettes
- Satin ribbon (⅛-inch wide in various colors; purchase spools at craft or fabric stores)
- Pony beads and feathers (optional)

Flower Loom
- Flower looms
- Yarn
- Scissors
- Plastic yarn needles

Quilling
- Quilling paper strips (can be ordered online)
- Thin, double-pointed knitting needles
- Glue sticks
- Card stock cut into bookmarks

ACTIVITIES

- Set up stations for each craft. After you demonstrate each craft, participants can move to the stations and try the crafts as desired.

- *Pom-Poms*: Wrap yarn over the cardboard strip, covering it thoroughly. Carefully slide the yarn off, tie it in the middle very tightly with another piece of yarn, cut, and fluff. The "DIY Cardboard Pom Pom Maker" page from *The Craft Train* blog provides helpful instructions for this method (https://www.thecrafttrain.com/diy-cardboard-pom-pom-maker/).

- *Macramé*: Print instructions for making basic macramé knots or copy some from a book in the library collection. Show audience members how to cut two long pieces of floss, knot each in the middle, and attach them to a safety pin, which will be clipped on the clipboard while patrons are working on the knots.

- *Ribbon Barrettes*: Cut two long strands of the ribbon and weave them across the parallel bars of the barrette to the end. Knot the ribbons underneath. Attach beads or feathers to the ends of the strands for an authentic vintage look. Instructions from XOJane may be helpful (https://www.xojane.com/diy/how-to-make-those-streamer-barrettes-from-your-70s-or-80s-childhood). This craft can also be used for the "'80s Accessories" program in the "1980s" chapter.

- *Flower Loom*: Demonstrate winding the yarn across the pegs of the flower loom, following package instructions or online guidance. When all pegs have been included, use a plastic needle and secure the middle before sliding the flower off the loom. The Underground Crafter instructions for this craft are especially easy to follow (https://www.youtube.com/watch?v=1Hjh3zxjtOc).

- *Quilling*: Copy some basic quilling shapes from library books or online sources. Wind the quilling paper strips around the thin needles. Apply some glue to the end of the bookmark to affix the coils. Have quilling books and patterns available so people can get ideas for shapes and projects.

MARKETING

- Display samples of the crafts to garner attention for the program.
- Offer drop-in events to test the crafts, such as pom-pom drop-ins after school.

VARIATIONS BY AGE GROUPS

- *Tweens, families*: Some easier crafts may attract these groups. For example, offer friendship bracelets instead of macramé (same supplies), or tissue paper and pipe cleaner flowers.

- *Tweens, families*: Offer each craft as a separate session in the summer for forty-five minutes each. Attendees can make pom-poms into animals, or tweens can make more elaborate crafts and learn more about each skill.

- *Seasonal crafts*: Add retro holiday crafts such as muslin angels, paper ornaments, holiday cards for charities, or items in holiday colors.

TIE-DYE

Although most fads from the '60s and '70s have faded over time, tie-dye remains a constant. This hands-on activity allows patrons to have a lot of fun creating something that is wholly unique.

PREP TIME	LENGTH OF PROGRAM	NUMBER OF PATRONS	SUGGESTED AGE RANGE
2 hours	1 hour	15	Tweens

SUPPLIES/SHOPPING

Tie-Dye
- White cotton T-shirts in various sizes (or ask patrons to bring in their own)
- Canvas tote bags, pillowcases, lunch bags, scarves, shoes, etc.
- Tie-dye kits (available at most craft stores)
- Rubber bands
- Latex-free gloves
- Plastic bags

Sharpie Tie-Dye T-Shirt
- Clean and dry white cotton T-shirt
- Sharpie permanent markers (various colors)
- Binder clips
- Iron
- Rubbing alcohol
- Eyedroppers
- Cardboard
- Hair dryer (optional)

Crayon Tie-Dye
- Crayons
- Glue
- Tape
- Hair dryers (2–3 if possible)
- Construction paper
- Cardboard

ACTIVITIES

- *Tie-Dye*: Have participants create or choose a pattern to use (patterns are easily found online; print out several ahead of time for patrons to choose from) and then demonstrate the following technique with a clean, dry white T-shirt. Twist or fold the shirt into the selected pattern and hold the shirt together with six to eight rubber bands. Wearing the gloves, squeeze the dye onto the shirt, with each section of the rubber bands marking a different color. Make sure that the shirt is saturated and that the dye goes into all the folds of the shirt. When participants have finished dyeing their shirts, place each shirt into a plastic bag for tweens to take home and wash.

- Choose a different item to tie-dye instead of a plain white T-shirt. Try tie-dyeing a canvas tote bag, pillowcases, lunch bags, scarves, or even shoes. Encourage patrons to bring in their own materials to tie-dye and personalize.

- *Sharpie Tie-Dye T-Shirt*: Try a unique method of tie-dye using Sharpie permanent markers. Insert cardboard in the middle of a clean white T-shirt so colors don't bleed through and apply designs to the shirt with Sharpies. Attach binder clips to pull the shirt taut on the sides and use an eyedropper to drip rubbing alcohol onto the ink design's center. The more drops you use, the larger the ink design will spread (don't oversaturate with the rubbing alcohol all at once). Let the T-shirt dry completely (if needed, use a hair dryer). Set the color into the shirt by applying the hot iron for five minutes on the highest heat. For instructions and a helpful video, see the "Sharpie Tie-Dye T-Shirt" page of Martha Stewart's website (https://www.marthastewart.com/892787/sharpie-tie-dye-t-shirt).

- *Crayon Tie-Dye*: Glue old crayons in designs onto a piece of construction paper. Keep the crayons very close together or arrange them in a row. Tape the construction paper onto a piece of cardboard to stabilize it and use a hair dryer to melt the crayons. Angle the cardboard in the direction you want the melting crayon to flow. When your masterpiece is completed, remove the tape and cardboard from the construction paper. Alternatively, tweens can create a drawing on the construction paper before attaching and melting the crayons.

MARKETING

Ask colleagues to bring in tie-dyed items that they own (blankets, shirts, etc.). Create a display with the items to advertise the program. If you would rather not use your own or anyone else's personal items, visit a local party store to pick up tie-dyed materials (wrapping paper, table decorations, etc.) to aid in creating the display. You can also check local thrift stores for tie-dyed items to use. The key is to make the display colorful and bright!

VARIATIONS BY AGE GROUPS

Tie-dye is a great all-ages craft and doesn't require much variation. If you want to hold separate tie-dye programs for different ages, consider selecting just one of the listed activities for each group.

PRO TIP

Be aware of primary and secondary colors because not all colors mix well. Blending certain colors together will produce brown.

Y.A., WHY NOT? THE GOLDEN AGE OF YOUNG ADULT LITERATURE

Current young adult titles are also popular with older readers. But those same adults may enjoy rereading young adult authors who were popular when the readers were teens. They can revisit favorite YA authors in this fun discussion series.

PREP TIME	LENGTH OF PROGRAM	NUMBER OF PATRONS	SUGGESTED AGE RANGE
45 minutes per session	4 sessions at 45 minutes each (some will run longer with movies)	18	Millennials, older adults

SUPPLIES/SHOPPING

- Laptop and projector (to show YouTube movies)
- Snacks and drinks (optional)
- Paper goods (optional)

ACTIVITIES

- Feature a different author each week. Participants can read any book from the '70s or '80s by these authors for the discussion. Each session will begin with participants introducing themselves and the book they read. Staff will give an overview of that week's author, including any awards and some trivia. Then everyone in the group will discuss memorable points, favorite quotes, reasons why the books have held up through the decades (or not), and favorite characters.

- *S. E. Hinton*: Show S. E. Hinton's interview on location during the filming of *The Outsiders* (https://www.youtube.com/watch?v=wJnfleLeOZg). After discussing the book, mention S. E. Hinton's age when she wrote the book and share some recent information about her, such as the fiftieth anniversary of *The Outsiders* in 2017 or posts from her Twitter feed. Show a clip from the *Outsiders* movie or the entire movie.

- *Judy Blume*: Show Rita Braver's 2015 interview with Judy Blume (https://www.youtube.com/watch?v=_KAAIschIBc). Discuss censorship and challenges of Judy Blume's books and how she supports those fighting challenges. A helpful source is "Protecting 'The Books That Will Never Be Written': Judy Blume's Fight Against Censorship" on the blog *A Mighty Girl* (https://www.amightygirl.com/blog?p=7425). After discussing the books, show clips from *Tiger Eyes* and *Forever*.

- *Lois Duncan*: Discuss Lois Duncan's career, and her recent investigation into her daughter's murder, to give perspective on her later life. Show a clip from one of the movies made of her books. Discuss any recent mystery, horror, or thriller authors who participants feel are similar and ask whether participants know of any recent young adult authors with a similar style.

- *Walter Dean Myers*: Discuss how Myers inspired the We Need Diverse Books movement (see http://weneeddiversebooks.org/we-need-diverse-books-announces-the-2017-walter-dean-myers-award-and-honor-books-for-outstanding-childrens-literature-young-adult-category/). Discuss whether books for young adults, in the opinion of participants, have become more diverse since Myers's earlier titles in the '70s and '80s. Show the interviews with Myers available on YouTube or in literature. Discuss how he followed up *Fallen Angels* about the Vietnam War with modern titles about relatives of those characters and recent military conflicts. Discuss his success with sports fiction for young adults, and consider which authors of adult materials may be as prolific as Myers.

MARKETING

Displays of the books by these authors with information about the series should be placed near adult fiction.

VARIATIONS BY AGE GROUPS

- *Teens*: *Oldies but Goodies*—Teen versions of this program may have read-alikes from current popular YA authors to bring relevance to the titles for today's teens.

- *Older adults*: *Young at Heart Book Discussion Group*—Older adults may enjoy some historical background about each of the authors, including pictures of the authors when they were young, what schools they went to, and details of their lives that may inspire memories in the older adults (for example, the clothing worn by the Greasers and Socs in *The Outsiders* or details of what life was like during the Vietnam War).

1980s

Only one of the authors of this book was young during the 1980s, yet all three of us are clearly passionate about that decade, which inspired us to create nine programs. From neon colors to fingerless gloves to leg warmers, the "'80s Accessories" program will help today's patrons easily bring back a bit of the decade to brighten their wardrobes. John Hughes movie fans will enjoy an "Attack of the Brat Pack." Other movie fans will appreciate being "Ghostbusted." "Graffiti Art" became its own genre in the '80s and now today's patrons will understand why. "I Want My MTV" revives some legendary music videos—and introduces them to young people. Changing gears for a food program, "Microwave Mania" updates some fast-cooking trends from the early days of home microwaves. Three toy and game programs round out the chapter. Who wouldn't want a "Pac-Man Party" or a "Rubik's Cube Challenge"? And if having fun with those classic toys and games isn't enough to satisfy patrons, they will return to learn about collecting crazes in the "Strawberry Shortcake, Cabbage Patch Kids, and Other Hot '80s Toys" program.

'80s ACCESSORIES

Although '80s fashion may not have been considered subtle, it certainly makes a statement. Many of these popular '80s accessories have reemerged today. Patrons can get trendy and start making their own fashion statements with a myriad of simple activities!

PREP TIME	LENGTH OF PROGRAM	NUMBER OF PATRONS	SUGGESTED AGE RANGE
3 hours	3 hours	40	Teens, millennials

SUPPLIES/SHOPPING

Everything Neon Headbands
- Cotton yoga headbands (can be purchased in bulk)
- Neon Sharpies or soft neon fabric paint
- Toothbrushes for splatter painting
- Large floor covering

Ribbon Barrettes
- Metal barrettes with two parallel bars, or split barrettes
- Satin ribbon (⅛-inch wide in several colors; buy inexpensively in rolls at craft or fabric stores)
- Pony beads and feathers (optional)

Leg Warmers
- Colorful knee-high socks (purchase in bulk)
- Fabric scissors

Fingerless Gloves
- Inexpensive lace or cloth gloves
- Fabric scissors

Plastic Geometric Earrings
- Plastic geometric shapes (available at toy or craft stores or on Amazon)
- Earring hooks
- Pliers (preferably jewelry pliers)
- Jump rings

Tutus
- Tulle (various colors)
- Scissors
- Ribbon
- Rulers

'80s T-Shirts
- T-shirts
- Fabric scissors

Scrunchies
- Elastic bands
- Safety pins
- Fabric in a variety of fun colors
- Hot glue gun and glue sticks
- Cloth tape measure

ACTIVITIES ···

- *Everything Neon Headbands*: Use neon Sharpies to add punk-style neon designs to stretchy headbands. Another option is to place the headbands on a large floor covering and splatter paint them using toothbrushes and neon paint. Allow enough time for the headbands to dry so patrons can pick them up and carry them home.

- *Ribbon Barrettes*: For instructions, see the "Retro Crafts" program in the "1970s" chapter.

- *Leg Warmers*: Leg warmers can be made by knitting or crocheting, or even by cutting off the sleeves of thrift store sweaters. Simple ones can be sewn using fleece and elastic. For the purposes of this '80s craft extravaganza, invite patrons to cut the toes off bulk knee-high socks to make instant leg warmers.

- *Fingerless Gloves*: Popular in the '80s, fingerless gloves are now handy for texting and playing video games. Michael Jackson made wearing one glove famous. Crafters can snip the fingers from purchased lace or fabric gloves to create this easy accessory.

- *Plastic Geometric Earrings*: Large, geometric-shaped earrings were all the rage in the '80s. Thread the geometric shapes, or a combination of them, through a jump ring and use the pliers to securely close the ring around the earring hook. To add more than one shape, use multiple jump rings.

- *Tutus*: These were a flash point in '80s fashion and have been brought back into the spotlight for 5Ks and other runs. Create unique, no-sew tutus out of tulle and ribbon (look for precut tulle to cut down on prep time). Wrap the ribbon around the waist of the person who is going to wear the tutu, making sure to overlap the ribbon, and tie it into a bow with about 10 inches left over. When cutting the tulle, remember that the finished tutu will be half as long as the piece of tulle (for example, if the tulle is 24 inches long, the tutu will be 12 inches long). Cut the tulle into 6-inch-wide pieces and loop each piece in half. Tuck the ends of the tulle around the ribbon and through the loop, pulling the tulle tight. Slide the pieces of tulle as close together as possible and continue to add to the tutu until it is full.

- *'80s T-Shirts*: Provide inexpensive T-shirts or suggest that patrons bring one in their own size to rip into *Flashdance* chic. An easy cut/slash-and-tie method can be found on the wikiHow website (https://www.wikihow.com/Make-a-80s -Style-Tee-Shirt). Men's T-shirts can be '80-ized by ripping the ribbed collars and sleeves off.

- *Scrunchies*: For instructions, see the "Attack of the Brat Pack" program.

MARKETING

- Invite nostalgic staff to wear some of the samples prior to the event.

- Make an eye-catching display with the samples. Include information about the program on the display.

VARIATIONS BY AGE GROUPS

- *Older adults*: Show *Flashdance* or *The Breakfast Club* while participants are working on the accessories.

- *Millennials*: Show *Desperately Seeking Susan, Full House, Punky Brewster, The Outsiders,* or '80s music videos while participants are making some of the matching accessories.

ATTACK OF THE BRAT PACK

For those born at a certain time, a trip down memory lane isn't complete without revisiting the works of, most notably, John Hughes and featuring a group of actors who in the '80s were referred to as the Brat Pack: Molly Ringwald, Anthony Michael Hall, Ally Sheedy, Rob Lowe, Emilio Estevez, Demi Moore, Andrew McCarthy, and Judd Nelson, as well as at various times a few others. Invite your Gen-X and millennial patrons to relive memories, or take your tween and teen patrons on a time travel adventure with a program celebrating '80s teen classics.

PREP TIME	LENGTH OF PROGRAM	NUMBER OF PATRONS	SUGGESTED AGE RANGE
4–5 hours	1½ hours (or longer, depending on movie showings)	25	Millennials, older adults

SUPPLIES/SHOPPING

- Elastic bands
- Safety pins
- Fabric in a variety of fun colors
- Hot glue gun and glue sticks
- Cloth tape measure
- Food and drinks (suggestions: Cool Ranch Doritos, Fruit-by-the-Foot, Gushers, Fruit Roll-Ups, Capri Sun)

ACTIVITIES

- *Costume Contest*: The look of the '80s is undeniable and unforgettable, so why not invite program attendees to dress as their favorite character from any of the memorable teen movies of the time and hold a costume contest?

- *'80s Prom*: Speaking of costumes, take a page out of *Pretty in Pink* and hold an '80s prom, complete with big hair and loud colors. Set up a photo booth to capture memories. Set up a dance floor and invite attendees to show off their *Thriller* moves and their pop-and-lock skills.

- *Crossover with the "I Want My MTV" Program*: Because this program is all things '80s, consider crossing it over with an "I Want My MTV" program or present each program separately as part of an '80s flashback week and promote one program during the other.

- *Movie Screenings*: Obviously a great route to take is to show any of the movies featuring the Brat Pack. The movie screening can be the main feature, or you can simply have one playing while other activities are going on.

CRANS

Scrunchies

- STEP 1: Depending on how thick you want the scrunchie to be, cut a piece of fabric between 15 and 20 inches long and 4 inches wide.

- STEP 2: Fold the piece of fabric in half the long way with the outside of the pattern (the brighter side) inside the fold.

- STEP 3: Glue the fabric together along the long edge, leaving about 2 inches unglued at either end. Wait for the glue to dry.

- STEP 4: Once the fabric is dry, turn it right side out.

- STEP 5: Bring the two ends together and glue. Make sure not to glue the openings from step 3. Let dry.

- STEP 6: While waiting for the glue to dry, attach safety pins to either end of an 8-inch-long piece of elastic.

- STEP 7: Once the glue is dry, feed the elastic through the loop until the two ends meet. Remove the safety pins.

- STEP 8: Glue the two ends of the elastic together.

- STEP 9: Glue the opening in the fabric closed.

- *Note*: If a sewing machine is available, all the gluing can be replaced with sewing. If patrons are gluing in lieu of using a sewing machine, have some needles and thread available for those who may want to hand sew their scrunchies in certain places for extra reinforcement.

TRIVIA AND OTHER FREE GAMES

Brat Pack Trivia: There is no shortage of trivia questions available for any or all of the movies that featured the Brat Pack, as well as questions about the actors themselves.

MARKETING

Create a display of movies featuring the Brat Pack and include on it information about the program. Also consider including on the display CDs of hits from the '80s. Position the display close to the AV materials.

VARIATIONS BY AGE GROUPS

For additional fun, consider crossing over with the "Pac-Man Party" program. This is a particularly good idea if the program is going to be held for tweens or teens or both, because it can be a true time warp for them!

GHOSTBUSTED

Who you gonna call? . . . The library, to have a fun *Ghostbusters*-themed program for your tween patrons! Ghostbusters, and ghosts, have long been part of the pop culture zeitgeist, and celebrating their moment in history is important. The 2016 reboot of *Ghostbusters* brought the paranormal ghost hunting gang back into the spotlight, with an emphasis on girl empowerment, female friendship, and women in science.

PREP TIME	LENGTH OF PROGRAM	NUMBER OF PATRONS	SUGGESTED AGE RANGE
2 hours	1 hour	20	Tweens

SUPPLIES/SHOPPING

Ecto Cooler
- 1 packet orange Kool-Aid or Flavor Aid
- 1 packet tangerine Kool-Aid or Flavor Aid
- ¾ cup orange juice (no pulp)
- ¾ cup tangerine juice or 1 can of mandarin oranges
- ⅓ scoop Country Time lemonade (regular or pink)
- 1½ cups sugar
- Green and blue food coloring
- Plastic cups
- Pitcher
- Large spoon

Slime
- Liquid starch
- Elmer's glue
- Sandwich bags
- Food dye
- Glitter (if desired)
- Water
- Measuring cups
- Plastic spoons
- Paper or plastic bowls
- Latex-free gloves

Marshmallow Structures
- Marshmallows (various colors and sizes)
- Toothpicks
- Paper plates

ACTIVITIES ···

- Have a paranormal investigation at the library. Measure the ghostly activity from a particular spooky spot in the library or near the 133s (parapsychology and occultism) using old children's light-up toys. Investigate hidden areas around the library and learn about the history of the library.

- Make Ecto Coolers! The peak of *Ghostbusters* deliciousness came in the form of the lime-green Ecto Cooler drink that was extremely popular as a lunchbox treat in the '90s. Re-create this drink using the official Ghostbusters: Chicago Division recipe (http://ghostbusterschicago.com/content/ecto-cooler-recipe).

- Invite a storyteller or talented librarian to tell ghost stories. Create a themed mood by dimming the lights, using a flashlight to illuminate the storyteller, and sitting on the floor.

- Of course, show one (or all) of the movies, if possible, either after the program or scheduled throughout the week.

CRAFTS ··

Slime
- Create *Ghostbusters* slime that will be sure to be a hit among tweens. Offer patrons latex-free gloves if they do not want to get their hands messy. Mix ½ cup water and ½ cup Elmer's glue in one bowl. Add food dye or glitter if desired (use light green to get the slime green color). Add ½ cup liquid starch into the mixture and begin to play with it to mold it in your hands. Switch the mixture to a dry bowl when all the water has been absorbed into the slime and it's not sticky. Tweens can transport their slime home in a sandwich bag, and it can stay viable up to a month in the refrigerator. Instructions and videos can be found on the *Little Bins for Little Hands* blog (http://littlebinsforlittlehands .com/liquid-starch-slime-easy-sensory-play-recipe/).

Detection Devices
- Tweens can design their own ghost detection gadget and become their own Jillian Holtzmann or Egon Spengler. Have tweens design a gadget to detect or fight off the paranormal using equipment or supplies from the library's craft or supply closet, or encourage imagination and have them draw their devices. Ask them to describe how their gadget would work and the science behind it.

Marshmallow Structures

- STEM up the program and have tweens create the Stay Puft Marshmallow Man out of toothpicks and marshmallows. Tweens can get creative and make other terrifying and hilarious villains out of marshmallows. Use multicolored marshmallows and different sizes for different effects.

TRIVIA AND OTHER FREE GAMES

Create trivia for the original *Ghostbusters* movie, the 2016 reboot, and classic ghost lore. Show clips from the movies and be sure to include visual and audio questions.

MARKETING

Create a cardboard cutout of the Stay Puft Marshmallow Man or Slimer. Cut out the face of the Marshmallow Man or Slimer so tweens can insert their faces and take pictures. Have the Marshmallow Man or Slimer hold a sign advertising the program day and time.

VARIATIONS BY AGE GROUPS

- *Teens*: Invite a local female scientist to talk about her experience in the workforce, her education, and any experiments that she is conducting. This is a great chance to expose teens to future career opportunities and to open up a discussion about what it means to be a woman in the science community today.

- *Millennials*: Age up your Ecto Cooler by incorporating different forms of alcohol, if your library has a liquor license. Expand the *Ghostbusters* theme of the program to include trivia from other popular ghost horror movies, such as *Poltergeist, Sixth Sense,* and *Paranormal Activity*.

- *Older adults*: Bring a speaker to the library to discuss local or state paranormal history. Go out into the community and organize a local ghost tour to explore your town. This is a great opportunity to partner with a local history museum or the chamber of commerce.

> **PRO TIP**
>
> **Check with your** local schools to see if they have a STEM club or a girls in science program. This is a great opportunity to partner for the program or to bring some of these activities to the schools.

GRAFFITI ART

From subway tunnels to the sides of buildings, graffiti art is inescapable. Gaining popularity as a means of cultural and social expression in the '80s, graffiti can be a way to express community spirit and values. Use graffiti as a unique art medium in your library programming and as a way to connect with your patrons.

PREP TIME	LENGTH OF PROGRAM	NUMBER OF PATRONS	SUGGESTED AGE RANGE
2 hours	1½ hours	15–20	Teens

SUPPLIES/SHOPPING

- DVDs or streaming capabilities of *Wild Style, Style Wars,* or *Exit Through the Gift Shop*
- DVD player or laptop (depending on technology setup)
- Projector and screen

Graffiti Art
- Foam core or poster board
- Plastic drop cloths or tarps
- Medium of choice: paint, spray paint
- Paintbrushes (if needed)
- Plastic cups (if needed)

Graffiti Art Medium Alternatives
- Rainworks spray (https://rain.works/)
- Cardboard or construction paper
- Scissors
- Sidewalk chalk

ACTIVITIES

- Invite a local graffiti artist to speak about the social and cultural history of graffiti in America and how graffiti has changed over the decades. Ask the speaker to demonstrate how he creates his artwork and formed his unique style.

- Show the documentary film *Style Wars* or the fictional film *Wild Style*. These movies are from the '80s, at the height of the graffiti renaissance. *Exit Through the Gift Shop* is another acclaimed documentary film about the famous street artist Banksy. Make sure you have the correct movie license before showing these films.

CRAFTS

Graffiti Art

- Have a freestyle graffiti session at the library and invite teens to create individual graffiti pieces to take home. Use large pieces of foam core or poster board and allow attendees to create large-scale pieces that express their own unique personality. Encourage them to fill up white space and to create their own tag (personalized signature), key components of becoming a graffiti artist.

- Design and create a graffiti art piece or mural for the library or teen area. This can be done either by working on the wall itself or by using several different pieces that fit together to create one complete artwork. Another alternative is to graffiti certain pieces in your teen spaces that you want to stand out, such as bookends, trash cans, or chairs. Determine some of the key components for the artwork ahead of time by having teens vote on what they want to include. This is a great project for a teen volunteer or art group—teens will feel valued and as if they were commissioned to work on a piece of art that can be featured for years to come.

- If your library is not ready to commit to having a full-blown mural in the public space, an alternative is to decorate the sidewalks around the library with a spray product called Rainworks that activates only when wet. Rainworks spray is invisible, repels water, and is active for two to three months. Teens cut out their designs on card stock or cardboard and use the Rainworks spray on the sidewalks. This is a fun, low-key project that will appear only when wet and is a great way to show art in an unexpected way.

MARKETING

- Use iconic graffiti images and font styles to create posters advertising your program.

- Share your teens' art processes and finished works on social media and your library website.

- Advertise your "Graffiti Art" program at art stores and local art studios to attract a new audience.

VARIATIONS BY AGE GROUPS

- *Tweens, millennials, older adults*: Sidewalk chalk on library siding and sidewalks can be a way to create temporary graffiti art. This can be a way to test the waters of collaborative art without committing to many years of permanent artwork.

- *All ages*: Invite your community to collaborate on a library-wide piece of graffiti art that will benefit the whole library. Hang it up proudly for everyone to enjoy and see.

PRO TIPS

If participants are working with spray paint, make sure the program is in a well-ventilated area. Encourage patrons to wear old clothing that they don't mind getting messy.

Talk with library administration before commissioning your teen advisory board to spray paint a mural. Spray paint may not be permitted or there may be limitations for the mural itself.

I WANT MY MTV

Whether you were alive when MTV premiered or were born long after the network stopped showing music videos, chances are you have at least a passing familiarity with MTV. Because the MTV of today bears little resemblance to the MTV of yesterday, it's the perfect candidate for a throwback program celebrating everything music television.

PREP TIME	LENGTH OF PROGRAM	NUMBER OF PATRONS	SUGGESTED AGE RANGE
2–3 hours	1 hour	25	Millennials

SUPPLIES/SHOPPING

Cassette Tape Pencil Holder
- Cassettes (4 per holder; can be found for very little money at thrift stores—stock up so you've got plenty for patrons to choose from)
- Sharp knife
- Hot glue gun and glue sticks
- Cardboard
- Scissors

CD Coasters
- CDs (as many as you want; these are also very inexpensive at thrift stores—stock up so you've got plenty to choose from)
- Felt
- X-acto knives
- Spray adhesive
- Acrylic paint (various colors)
- Card stock (various colors)
- Markers
- Contact paper (clear)
- Sandpaper

ACTIVITIES

- *Thriller Dance-Off*: Bring interested participants together to try their moves in the iconic dance featured in Michael Jackson's *Thriller* video.

- *Breakdancing*: Throw down some flattened cardboard boxes and invite participants to try out their breaking skills.

- *Crossover with TR-Not-So-L*: The activities outlined in the "TR-Not-So-L" program in the "2000s" section of this book can be incorporated into this program. Or you can present these two as separate programs and promote one at the other.

CRAFTS

Cassette Tape Pencil Holder
(For instructions and helpful photos, see the Upcycle That website at https://www.upcyclethat.com/upcycled-cassettes/2297/).

- STEP 1: The edges on the sides of the tapes have bumps or "guides" for positioning the cassette tape correctly in the player. Using a sharp knife, scrape off these bumps.

- STEP 2: Place four cassette tapes in a box shape and glue the edges of the four cassettes together.

- STEP 3: To make the base, place the cassette structure on a piece of cardboard and trace around it.

- STEP 4: Cut out the cardboard base and glue it to the cassette structure.

CD Coasters

- STEP 1: Decide whether you want to be able to see the design on the CD (perhaps if it has nostalgic value) or want to paint or cover it.

- STEP 2: If you want to leave the design visible, lay the CD design-side down on a piece of clear contact paper and use an X-acto knife to trace around it, cutting out an appropriate piece of contact paper. Attach the contact paper to the design side of the CD. This will help to protect it against moisture.

- STEP 3: If you want to decorate the design side of the CD, use the sandpaper to gently sand off the coating.

- STEP 4: Lay the CD design-side down on a piece of card stock and use the X-acto knife to cut out a piece of card stock. Use the markers to color or draw a design on the card stock. Consider providing stencils for patrons to use if they'd rather not draw freehand.

- STEP 5: Use spray adhesive to affix the card stock to the design side of the CD.

- STEP 6: Apply contact paper as in step 2.

- STEP 7: Lay the CD down on a piece of felt and use the X-acto knife to trace around the CD, cutting out an appropriately sized piece of felt.

- STEP 8: Spray one side of the felt with the spray adhesive and attach it to the shiny side of the CD.

TRIVIA AND OTHER FREE GAMES

MTV's cultural reach was far and wide throughout the '80s and '90s, making it a perfect candidate for a trivia contest. You can skip writing questions and use Trivial Pursuit Pop Culture Edition or a similar product.

MARKETING

Create a display of CDs and books about popular music acts that would have been on MTV, and include on the display information about the program.

VARIATIONS BY AGE GROUPS

Tweens, teens: Add a portable green screen and let tweens and teens try out their VJ skills!

MICROWAVE MANIA

Though microwave ovens were invented in the 1940s and began being used in domestic kitchens in the late 1960s, they really came into their own in the 1980s, with new gadgets and recipes and microwaveable foods appearing everywhere. If you don't have access to at least three or four microwave ovens, demonstrate some popular '80s microwaveable foods and then serve portions for audience members to taste.

PREP TIME	LENGTH OF PROGRAM	NUMBER OF PATRONS	SUGGESTED AGE RANGE
2 hours	1½ hours	20–25	Tweens, teens, millennials, older adults, families

SUPPLIES/SHOPPING

- Plates
- Forks

- Napkins
- Cups (for water)

French Toast
- Egg
- Milk
- Cinnamon
- Vanilla

- Bread (2 loaves)
- Syrup
- Microwave-safe plate

Bacon
- Bacon

- Microwave-safe plate

Cheese and Salsa Dip
- Microwave-safe bowl
- Velveeta cheese (2 16-ounce bricks)

- Salsa (large jar)
- Tortilla chips (large size)
- Spoons

Microwaveable Popcorn
- Microwave popcorn packets
- Variety of spices and add-ins for flavors, including chili, white chocolate chips
- Microwave-safe bowls for cooking, flavoring

Stouffer's Frozen French Bread Pizza
- Stouffer's Frozen French Bread Pizza
- Knife

ACTIVITIES

- *French Toast*: An easy recipe for microwave French toast can be found on the Genius Kitchen website (www.geniuskitchen.com/recipe/microwave-french-toast-433816).

- *Bacon*: Show how easy it can be to make bacon in the microwave using the instructions on the Food Network website (www.foodnetwork.com/recipes/articles/how-to-make-bacon-in-the-microwave).

- *Cheese and Salsa Dip*: Cut the Velveeta into cubes and pour the salsa over them in the bowl before microwaving. Spoon over tortilla chips on tasting plates.

- *Microwave Popcorn Plus Flavors*: Make microwave popcorn and offer spices and other add-ins so participants can flavor their servings. Some easy, healthy flavorings can be found on Pinterest (https://www.pinterest.com/pin/537969117970775904/).

- *Stouffer's Frozen French Bread Pizza*: An '80s favorite, this food can now be made in the microwave. It is a good choice for cutting into portions and serving to audience members.

TRIVIA AND OTHER FREE GAMES

Show photos or gadgets for microwave cooking, including ones for fixing bacon, cooking eggs, baking, and more, and see if anyone in the audience can identify them—or has used them.

MARKETING

- Catch patrons' attention with signs and electronic banners that feature the word *food*!

- Offer samples of microwaved foods for tasting and include information about the program.

VARIATIONS BY AGE GROUPS

Millennials: Show the movie *Real Genius* while making different flavors of microwave popcorn (though, of course, they don't use a microwave in the movie!).

> **PRO TIP**
>
> **If you have** three or four microwaves available, encourage groups of four to five participants to make and share each food during the class.

PAC-MAN PARTY

Give your patrons an opportunity to celebrate the nostalgia of Friday nights at the arcade with a Pac-Man party! You can celebrate all things 8-bit by including other arcade games, too.

PREP TIME	LENGTH OF PROGRAM	NUMBER OF PATRONS	SUGGESTED AGE RANGE
3–4 hours	1–1½ hours	25	Millennials

SUPPLIES/SHOPPING

Classic Pac-Man
- Namco Museum Virtual Arcade for Xbox 360
- Television(s)

Live Pac-Man
- Construction paper or card stock (yellow, orange, pink, red, turquoise, white)
- Scissors
- Markers
- Hole punch
- Yarn
- Masking or painter's tape
- Small blocks or toys (25–30; optional—you can also use crushed up balls of paper)

Pac-Man Picture Frames
- Inexpensive wood picture frames (various sizes; check thrift stores and dollar stores)
- Acrylic paint (black, white, yellow, blue, pink, orange, turquoise, red, green)
- Paintbrushes (various widths)

Pac-Man Perler Beads
- Perler beads (yellow, orange, pink, red, blue, turquoise, white, black)
- Iron
- Pac-Man Perler bead patterns (available online)
- Pegboards (clear)
- Parchment paper

ACTIVITIES ···

- *Classic Pac-Man*: If your library system owns a copy (or more than one) of Namco Museum Virtual Arcade (or if you are able to purchase or borrow a copy), set up a gaming station where patrons can enjoy testing their Pac-Man skills.

- *Live Pac-Man*: These instructions have been modified from the blog *If You Loved . . .* (http://bit.ly/2wsbjtg).

  » STEP 1: Set up your playing area. Make a Pac-Man out of the yellow construction paper and make each of the four ghosts out of the remaining colors. You can print out templates online and simply trace and cut out each one. Use the white paper for the ghosts' eyes. Use the string and hole punch to make each one into a necklace so participants can wear their character around their neck and be easily identifiable during the game.

  » STEP 2: Using the masking or painter's tape, create a Pac-Man grid on the floor of the room in which you'll be playing. You'll need a fairly large room, or at least a lot of floor space, to play Live Pac-Man. Examples of floor grids can be found online.

  » STEP 3: The dots on the grid (i.e., what Pac-Man "eats") can be created by using small wooden blocks or other small toys or by just wadding up paper. Because Pac-Man needs to be able to pick up the items, you'll have to use something other than tape. Consider also giving Pac-Man a small bag to put all the tokens in as they are picked up.

  » STEP 4: Designate one participant to be Pac-Man and four participants to be the ghosts—Inky (turquoise), Blinky (red), Pinky (pink), and Clyde (orange). The program leader will announce when each person may enter as well as each time a change in play occurs.

    a. To begin, have the ghosts stand in the center of the grid. Pac-Man will enter from one of the sides.
    b. Players must waddle penguin-style while navigating the maze, keeping their legs together.
    c. Pac-Man enters the maze first to begin collecting tokens. After a few seconds (five to seven or so), the program leader will announce that the first ghost may enter. The ghosts continue to enter the maze at five- to seven-second intervals.
    d. The ghosts' objective is to tag Pac-Man. Pac-Man has three lives, and each tag will result in the loss of one life. Each time Pac-Man is tagged, the ghosts return to the center and have to be released again. Pac-Man may stay in place and continue collecting tokens when the game is back in play.

e. When Pac-Man picks up a Power Pellet (located in each corner of the grid), the program leader announces that all ghosts currently in play must move backward. Ghosts are not allowed to tag Pac-Man while they are moving backward, but Pac-Man can tag them. If a ghost is tagged, that player must return to the center of the grid and wait to be released again. Ghosts move backward for ten seconds, after which the program leader announces that they can once again move forward.

f. When Pac-Man has been tagged three times, the game is over and the pieces are reset for the next group.

CRAFTS

Pac-Man Picture Frames

- STEP 1: Remove the glass and backing from each frame.

- STEP 2: Paint each frame black.

- STEP 3: Once the black paint has dried completely, add the Pac-Man grid. Include the following items on the grid:

  » Small white dots for the Pac-Dots
  » Large white dots for the Power Pellets
  » A yellow Pac-Man
  » Any of the four ghosts in their "normal" state
  » Ghosts in their edible state
  » Fruit (strawberry, cherry, orange)

Pac-Man Perler Beads

To give patrons a chance to have their very own 8-bit Pac-Man, set up a Perler bead station. Pac-Man Perler bead patterns can be found online, and detailed information about working with Perler beads can be found on wikiHow (www .wikihow.com/Use-Perler-Beads).

TRIVIA AND OTHER FREE GAMES

Patrons are already showing off their Pac-Man skills, so why not also have them show off their classic arcade game knowledge?

MARKETING

If you've got the time, set up a mini Live Pac-Man grid to catch patrons' attention. You can even make some of the characters out of construction paper and include them on a table near the grid with information about the program.

VARIATIONS BY AGE GROUPS

Variations aren't necessary. Pac-Man can be enjoyed by all ages!

PRO TIPS

Because the paint will need time to dry, paint several (or all, depending on how many you have and what your preference is) of the frames black ahead of time (steps 1 and 2). That way, patrons can get right to painting their Pac-Man scene.

Print off pictures of Pac-Man games and have them available for patrons to reference when painting their own grids.

RUBIK'S CUBE CHALLENGE

Since its 1974 invention by Erno Rubik, the cube puzzle has remained popular. Many variations exist, along with records on solving speeds. Invite cube enthusiasts to this fun event where they can learn tricks for solving the cube more quickly, race other players, and even make their own photo cubes.

PREP TIME	LENGTH OF PROGRAM	NUMBER OF PATRONS	SUGGESTED AGE RANGE
2 hours	2 hours	20	Tweens, teens, families

SUPPLIES/SHOPPING

- Mini Rubik's Cubes (either the 2x2 size, or the small version of the classic 3x3; 22, which includes 1 for the instructor and a spare in case of breakage)
- Timer
- Prizes (pencils, puzzles; optional)

Photo Cubes
- Many small, colorful images on label paper
- Mini cubes
- Rulers
- Pencils
- Scissors

2x2, 3x3, 4x4 (optional)
- Several 2x2, 3x3, and 4x4 cubes

ACTIVITIES

- *Solving Strategies*: Offer YouTube or printed instructions on ways to solve the cubes and let players try to do it as they arrive. One popular source is Ruwix, the Rubik's Cube wiki (https://ruwix.com/the-rubiks-cube/how-to-solve-the-rubiks-cube-beginners-method/). Invite those who are successful at solving the cube to show others what they did.

- *Timed Challenges*: Once some participants are comfortable solving the cube, have a timed challenge among three or four participants.

- *2x2, 3x3, 4x4*: Pass around different types of cubes and invite groups to take turns trying to solve them.

CRAFTS

Photo Cubes

- Before the event, print several colorful images on label paper. The images should be slightly bigger than a side of a small Rubik's Cube.

- As participants finish the timed challenge, invite them to select six images on the label papers. With a pencil, make grids on the images that match the sides of the cubes. (If the side is 3x3 ½-inch cubes, then the paper should be marked the same way.)

- Cut the mini squares one row at a time (so puzzles will not be mixed up) and apply right over the squares on the mini cubes.

TRIVIA AND OTHER FREE GAMES

Set up a couple of laptops so participants can take the Rubik's Cube quiz while waiting for a turn or a challenge (https://ruwix.com/the-rubiks-cube/rubiks-cube-quiz/).

MARKETING

Have a Rubik's Cube available at each service desk in the library to advertise the program. When patrons pick it up to play, tell them about the program.

VARIATIONS BY AGE GROUPS

Millennials, older adults: Some of these activities could be part of a 1980s party with millennials or older adults.

STRAWBERRY SHORTCAKE, CABBAGE PATCH KIDS, AND OTHER HOT '80s TOYS

By the end of 1983, people were fighting over Xavier Roberts's Cabbage Patch Kids in stores. It was the beginning of modern holiday must-have toy crazes. But several items emerged from the '80s as highly collectible. Take audience members on a nostalgic trip through decades past with a presentation, or invite them to display collections.

PREP TIME	LENGTH OF PROGRAM	NUMBER OF PATRONS	SUGGESTED AGE RANGE
2 hours	2 hours	50	Millennials, older adults

SUPPLIES/SHOPPING

Rainbow Brite Coloring Station
- Markers
- Rainbow Brite coloring sheets (www.coloringpages101.com/Cartoons/Rainbow-Brite-coloring-pages)

Strawberry Shortcake
- Squares of pound cake
- Whipped cream (in aerosol cans)
- Strawberries (cut into halves)
- Plates or bowls
- Napkins
- Forks and spoons

He-Man/Jem Drawing Station
- Pencils
- Paper

Prizes (optional)
- Rubik's Cubes, collector cards for any of the discussed toys, and the like

ACTIVITIES ···

- *Collector Fair*: Invite participants to register to show their collections at a table during the program. After patrons watch the presentation and overview of some hot collectibles, invite patrons to browse the tables or play trivia games.

- *Strawberry Shortcake*: Describe these dolls and their modern variations. Design games in which attendees match the flavor to the doll name or match the pet to the doll. Show the introduction from one of the 1980s television specials and photos of the mini dolls. Show photos of other toys connected with this collection and some of the modern versions. Invite participants to put together their own strawberry shortcake from pound cake, whipped cream, and strawberries.

- *Cabbage Patch Kids*: Describe the Cabbage Patch Kids craze and elements of the dolls, such as the sculpted body, the signature, and the adoption certificate. Describe the high prices that original models currently command at auction, and discuss the different variations of dolls, clothes, and gear. Show photos of different tags and certificates. Compare Cabbage Patch Kids to the American Girl dolls. Put several Cabbage Patch Kid names (available online) in a bowl and invite people to choose new names for themselves.

- *Fisher-Price Little People*: Set up some vintage and modern Little People toys for display if possible. Show photos of older toys as well as modern variations and discuss pricing and unusual items to collect. The Fisher-Price Collectors Club website has great historical information (www.fpclub.org/littlepeople.html).

- *Rainbow Brite*: Discuss the history and variations of Rainbow Land and its inhabitants. *Hint*: One collector has a museum (https://www.rainbowbrite.net/collectibles.html)! Have markers and Rainbow Brite coloring sheets available at tables for a few minutes of relaxation.

- *Garbage Pail Kids*: Show photos and discuss the history of these unpleasant hot items from the '80s. Invite patrons to invent new Garbage Pail Kid names and write them on scraps of paper. Then pull one or more names for a prize.

- *'80s Action Figures*: Briefly discuss the worlds of He-Man, She-Ra, and Jem as well as modern variations of these toys. Show a clip from a *He-Man and the Masters of the Universe,* a *She-Ra: Princess of Power,* or a *Jem* TV program. Invite people to draw any of the He-Man or Jem characters within five minutes.

- *Rubik's Cube*: Have some cubes available for people to play with. Briefly mention the history of the cube during the presentation. See also the "Rubik's Cube Challenge" program earlier in this chapter.

- *Care Bears*: Show the history of the Care Bears and modern variations of the characters.

TRIVIA AND OTHER FREE GAMES

- *Fisher-Price Little People*: Instead of trivia, invite people to vote on their favorite building from the Fisher-Price Little People collection, either on paper with a description or at a laptop with photos.

- *'80s Action Figures*: Have a contest in which participants match the character to the name.

MARKETING

Invite local collectors to display some '80s collectibles, such as the Rubik's Cube or Fisher-Price Little People, in a locked case, or display some at reference desks along with information about the program.

VARIATIONS BY AGE GROUPS

Millennials: Show episodes from *Jem, He-Man,* or other '80s kids' hits. Invite people to bring toys and have an expert appraise them for value.

1990s

Although perhaps not as colorful as the neon 1980s, the 1990s sowed the seeds of change in music, technology, and fashion. A "'90s Technology and Game Night" will allow people to remember Nintendo and Walkman devices and why they were so enjoyable. Vests and other accessories defined some years in the '90s, and "Flair Fun" will inspire fashionistas of today. Flannel was another '90s staple, and the "Flannel Pillows" program invites people to easily create cuddly accessories for the home—even those who don't know how to sew! We celebrated the 1950s with an "I Love Lucy" program, and we will remember the 1990s with a "Nickelodeon Nostalgia Night." "Boy Bands and Girl Power!" were everywhere in the 1990s, and many of those same stars are still in the entertainment industry. Music lovers will enjoy revisiting those classics or others in the "Riot Grrrl Celebration" program saluting punk. The 1990s produced enough different styles and types of entertainment for everyone to enjoy.

'90S TECHNOLOGY AND GAME NIGHT

Technology is always advancing and pushing us to be the best and brightest. Remember when the coolest thing on the block was a Nintendo Game Boy or a Walkman? Let's go back to the '90s and party like it's 1999!

PREP TIME	LENGTH OF PROGRAM	NUMBER OF PATRONS	SUGGESTED AGE RANGE
2–3 hours	1 hour	15–20	Tweens

SUPPLIES/SHOPPING

'90s Tech ID
- Ask your coworkers to dig through their closets and donate their old '90s toys, games, and technology (for example, pagers, Talkboys, answering machines, cassette players, VHS tapes, Tamagotchis, etc.)
- Paper
- Pencils

'90s Game Night
- '90s games (see suggestions in the activities section)
- Paper
- Pencils

Take-Apart Night
- Items to take apart (old computers, Nintendo systems, pagers, Game Boys, PalmPilots, Zip drives, etc.)
- Screwdrivers
- Gloves

ACTIVITIES

- *'90s Tech ID*: Set out an assortment of individual items of '90s technology, such as a PalmPilot, pager, Zip drive, and the like, and label each with a number. Ask patrons to identify each item and tell what it does. If participants don't know, that's even better! Have them think of unique and original names and descriptions of what each device might do. After telling them what each device really does, give attendees the opportunity to play with each piece of technology and speculate about how it evolved . . . or didn't.

- *'90s Game Night*: Play old-school, '90s handheld, computer, video, or board games. Ask staff members to donate theirs for the program, or scavenge secondhand stores. Tell tweens to put away all their twenty-first-century devices and get a true glimpse into what life was really like in the '90s. Teach them how to play MASH, how to play cat's cradle, and how to create a cootie catcher. Examples of '90s games include Super Mario Bros., Oregon Trail (available now as a board game), Tiger handheld games, and Pogs.

- *Take-Apart Night*: Have participants dissect the insides of an old Apple computer or a Nintendo 64 system that doesn't work. Many libraries often have older computers or technology from many years ago when they last upgraded their systems. This is a chance to recycle old technology and collaborate with other departments. Work with your computer assistance or technology department to teach patrons about the basic parts of the computer and how it has adapted and changed since the '90s.

TRIVIA AND OTHER FREE GAMES

If you don't have access to a lot of '90s-specific technology, you can easily produce a '90s technology trivia night. Create a PowerPoint or *Jeopardy!*-style presentation based on '90s games or technology. Expand on this theme by including other categories such as toys or clothing and present a whole '90s trivia night!

MARKETING

Advertise this program with a rad '90s-themed flyer in your technology or children's section or near the children's computers. Use bright, neon colors and add a few pictures of '90s technology you will be using.

VARIATIONS BY AGE GROUPS

- *Teens, older adults*: Reverse the '90s technology identification game. Have teens teach the latest technology to older adults, potentially earning volunteer hours if allowed.

- *Tweens, teens, older adults*: Host an intergenerational gaming night and pair a younger tween or teen with an older adult to play old-school games.

PRO TIP

If patrons will be taking apart a computer, check with your IT or computer assistance department about removing potentially hazardous pieces before patrons access them.

FLAIR FUN

The 1999 movie *Office Space* featured a young woman whose job uniform of a vest or suspenders was to be covered with pieces of "flair," or decorations. Vests were popular fashion accessories in the '90s, and people personalized them in many ways. This program will allow fashion decoration or instruction in making easy, no-sew vests.

PREP TIME	LENGTH OF PROGRAM	NUMBER OF PATRONS	SUGGESTED AGE RANGE
2 hours	1 hour for decoration, 1½ hours if participants are making vests	20	Tweens, teens, millennials

SUPPLIES/SHOPPING

Flair

- Vests or T-shirts (purchase in bulk in large and extra-large sizes, or ask participants to provide their own)
- Mini slogan pins (purchase in bulk)
- Sharpies or fabric markers
- Fabric glue
- Ribbon or lace bits (or spools of ribbon and lace)
- Fabric flowers
- Swarovski crystals
- Fabric paints, brushes

Making Vests

- Used jeans, knit fabrics, or wool felt (or suede cloth or other fabrics that do not fray)
- Fabric scissors
- Measuring tapes
- Pins
- Rotary cutters
- Cutting boards
- Butcher paper—or large sheets (for the wool felt vest)

ACTIVITIES

- *Flair*: Show photos or discuss different decoration options before allowing participants to decorate vests or T-shirts.

- *Making Vests*: Choose one of the following options.

  » *From jeans*: Have participants bring a pair of old jeans that fits them to turn into a vest. A video from BlueprintDIY has easy-to-follow instructions (https://www.youtube.com/watch?v=LUq2N7s2B6M&feature=share).

» *From knit fabric*: Requiring only one yard of knit fabric, these no-sew vests are easy. Find instructions on the *One Little Momma* blog (www.onelittle momma.com/2012/10/easy-knit-vest-tutorial-no-sew.html).

» *From wool felt or suede cloth*: Making an easy vest from wool felt, suede cloth, or other fabric that does not fray will not take long. Instructions can be found on eHow (www.ehow.com/how_12068039_make-nosew -vest-out-felt.html).

CRAFTS

Shoe Flair
- If patrons bring in plain canvas shoes, they can decorate with markers, crystals, lace, ribbons, and paints. Shoelaces can be replaced with ribbons for effect.

MARKETING

- Encourage staff members to wear decorated clothing or display some pieces to advertise the event.

- Put trivia from '90s movies including *Office Space* on a bookmark along with information about the program.

VARIATIONS BY AGE GROUPS

- *Families*: Invite families to bring in their own vests, T-shirts, and plain canvas shoes to decorate. Have stations with crystals, lace and ribbons, paints, and other embellishments and let participants decorate at will. Display photos for ideas.

- *Millennials, older adults*: Show the movie *Office Space* before the event (because it is rated R).

PRO TIP

Because this program could require the purchase of fabric, it might be advisable to give participants a list of supplies and let them buy their own, or request a small deposit to offset the cost of the program.

FLANNEL PILLOWS

Flannel was everywhere in the 1990s, from clothing to decor. Sewing and craft classes are popular at libraries, and making pillows is a good beginner sewing project. No-sew options are also available for this craft event.

PREP TIME	LENGTH OF PROGRAM	NUMBER OF PATRONS	SUGGESTED AGE RANGE
1½ hours	1½ hours	15	Teens, millennials, older adults

SUPPLIES/SHOPPING

- Several scraps of flannel in ½-yard increments
- Fabric scissors
- Straight pins
- Cutting boards
- Rotary cutters
- Plastic cutting guides for fabric
- Chalk or fabric marking pencils
- Sewing and shirt options: hand sewing needles, thread in gray and black, stuffing or bulk cotton batting to fold inside pillows—or inexpensive travel-sized pillows
- Large buttons for decoration (optional)
- Fusing option: at least three irons, ironing boards (mini ones will work), fusible bonding web strips, pressing cloth (cotton knit works well)
- Gluing option: fabric glue
- Used flannel shirts (purchase from thrift or bargain stores or ask patrons to bring their own)

ACTIVITIES

- There are several ways to make pillows, including some no-sew ways. If sewing machines are available, consider offering more advanced designs for those who are old enough and are familiar with using a machine. Choose a method ahead of time—either hand sewing, gluing, or fusing with the iron and bonding web. The number of participants for this program will be determined by the equipment and staff available. Consider offering the program more than once if the topic is popular.

- *Flannel Fold-over*: Cut 12-by-18-inch squares of flannel. Sew (or glue or fuse) two seams to make into a tube, with a fold on one long side, and one end open. Stuff. Fold in the edge of the open side so 2 inches of fabric are folded inside the pillow. Seal the edge or hand sew some decorative buttons along the edge to do so.

- *Patchwork*: Cut four 3-inch squares of flannel in mismatched colors. Show participants how to attach two sets of two squares, then put them together so the middle cross seams match up to form a four-square design. Cut a backing of flannel to fit the top, then seal three sides. Stuff. Seal the fourth side.

- *Flannel Shirts*: Cut, fold, and sew a flannel shirt into a cute covering for a small pillow or travel pillow. Helpful directions are available from the *Happy at Home* blog (http://robin-happyathome.blogspot.com/2013/11/from-flannel-shirt-to-pillow-cover.html).

- *Scrunchies*: Make flannel scrunchies with a scrap of flannel and elastic. This is a good hand sewing project. For instructions, see the "Attack of the Brat Pack" program in the "1980s" chapter.

MARKETING

Place flannel pillows on prominent chairs, with tags about the program pinned to the pillows.

VARIATIONS BY AGE GROUPS

- *Millennials*: When patrons register for the program, mention that a loudest print or most worn flannel shirt contest will be part of the event. Offer small prizes and take photos for library social media.

- *Families*: In addition to one type of pillow, families may enjoy making flannel blankets. Provide 2 yards of plaid or checked flannel for each family registered for the event. Cut approximately 2½-inch fringe (use the pattern of checks or plaid on the flannel as your guide), about ¼- to ⅓-inch wide, all the way around the fabric. Family members can work on opposite sides, but caution them that fabric scissors are very sharp. The fringe will fray after washing, adding to a cozy, rustic look for the blanket.

- *Holiday*: Offer flannels in holiday colors or even heart shapes as a themed choice.

NICKELODEON NOSTALGIA NIGHT

Often thought of as the golden age of television programming for children, the 1990s ushered in television dominated by dedicated children's television shows. Nickelodeon was one of the first television networks dedicated solely to children's programming, with shows ranging from game shows to scary stories and beyond. Nickelodeon was part of many millennials' formative childhood years, and they will immediately recognize key pieces and imagery from Nickelodeon shows that will invoke waves of nostalgic feelings. Use this phenomenon to amp up your programming and catch the eye of millennials who will recognize such iconic pieces as the Shrine of the Silver Monkey from *Legends of the Hidden Temple,* the Giant Eye from *What Would You Do?* and the campfire from *Are You Afraid of the Dark?* Re-create games and programs based on popular '90s Nickelodeon shows, either as a multi-event program or a solo program.

PREP TIME	LENGTH OF PROGRAM	NUMBER OF PATRONS	SUGGESTED AGE RANGE
3–4 hours	1–2 hours	25–50 (depending on space and activities)	Millennials

SUPPLIES/SHOPPING

Legends of the Hidden Temple
- Noisemakers
- Timer
- Card stock or cardboard
- Duct tape
- Challenge supplies (as determined by programmer; see suggestions in the activities section)

Double Dare
- Challenge supplies (as determined by programmer; see suggestions in the activities section)
- Whiteboard
- Dry-erase markers

Are You Afraid of the Dark?
- Toaster oven or microwave
- Marshmallows
- Graham crackers
- Chocolate bars
- Paper plates
- Napkins
- Scary story library books
- *Are You Afraid of the Dark?* DVD
- DVD player, laptop, or projector and screen

Salute Your Shorts
- Outdoor games of choice (as determined by programmer; see suggestions in the activities section)
- Lined paper
- Pens or pencils
- Blank journals
- Guitar or ukulele
- Dream catcher kits
- Embroidery floss
- Scissors
- Tape
- Posterboard
- Puff paint or fabric markers
- T-shirts
- Armbands or headbands

ACTIVITIES

Legends of the Hidden Temple
- Before the program, create the Shrine of the Silver Monkey out of card stock or cardboard and duct tape. Instructions can be found on the DeviantArt website (https://billybob884.deviantart.com/art/Silver -Monkey-Assembled-93583244).

- Re-create *Legends of the Hidden Temple* challenges such as assembling the Shrine of the Silver Monkey, completing the Steps of Knowledge, and competing in the Temple Games. The Steps of Knowledge is a trivia challenge: choose one team member to compete in each round of trivia (one question in each round). Two out of three correct answers moves that team to the next round. Use different types of noisemakers as buzzers to determine who signaled first. The teams with the most points move on to the next round and get ready to assemble the Shrine of the Silver Monkey. Move to another programming room and instruct one team to find three hidden pieces of the Shrine of the Silver Monkey (base, body, head) and assemble it in order. Alternatively, give each team clues to decipher to find the pieces within the room, which is helpful if rooms are limited. The final teams get to compete in the Temple Games, which is a series of physical challenges. These can be as creative or physically competitive as your library allows, from doing the limbo to completing the most push-ups in a given time to finishing an obstacle course. If there is a tie at the end of the games, ask a tiebreaker trivia question to determine the winner.

Double Dare

- Double Dare is a partnered game of wild, wacky, and potentially messy challenges. Create trivia questions before the program and determine wacky challenges for partners to do. Trivia can be general knowledge, and if one of the teams takes the dare, the other team has to answer the question or take the challenge. Points are earned for each challenge or trivia question, and games can be played to the librarian's chosen value. Keep track of teams' scores and dares on a whiteboard for participants and audience members. Challenges are the librarian's choice (some examples follow).

- Begin by explaining the rules of the game: "I'm going to ask you a question, and if you don't know the answer, or think the other team hasn't got a clue, you can dare them to answer it for double the dollars (or points). But be careful, because they can always double dare you back for four times the amount (or points) and then you either have to answer that question or take the physical challenge." Although teams won't be wagering real money, use a point system to determine question values.

- Physical challenges can range from fun to ridiculous. Examples include the following:
  - » *Pop It*: Blow up an assortment of balloons in different colors and let them go throughout the room. Teams are assigned a balloon color and must pop all the balloons by sitting on them. The first team to finish popping all their designated color balloons wins.
  - » *Mail Delivery*: Teams throw paper airplanes into a mailbox from a set distance (substitute a cardboard box for a mailbox if needed). The first team to get an airplane in the mailbox wins the challenge.
  - » *Word Scramble*: Using large, precut letters, teams create four words that are four letters or longer. The team that makes four words the quickest wins.
  - » *Mousetrap*: Teams launch slices of cheese across the room onto an oversize mousetrap or bowl. The first team to get four slices onto the mousetrap wins the challenge.

Are You Afraid of the Dark?

- The show *Are You Afraid of the Dark?* involved a group of teenagers who called themselves the Midnight Society and who would meet to tell a scary story around a campfire. This program is a chance to highlight the library's collection of horror stories and show off a librarian's talent at storytelling. Encourage patrons to participate and share their own stories, even if they aren't scary. Create a faux campfire and provide s'mores supplies and a microwave or toaster oven to heat marshmallows and chocolate bars. Show a classic episode of *Are You Afraid of the Dark?* as well.

Salute Your Shorts

- Meet up once again with the Camp Anawanna gang and relive the antics of summer camp at the library. Play outdoor games such as capture the flag and cornhole (or bean bag toss), write letters home to family, and jam out on a guitar or ukulele around a campfire (real or imaginary). If possible, hold the program off-site at a nature or recreation center and enjoy the great outdoors.

CRAFTS

- Patrons can create team T-shirts, armbands, and headbands to show solidarity for their team. Provide quick-drying puff paint or fabric markers for patrons to decorate their shirts or for their cheering squad to create posters.

- During the "Salute Your Shorts" summer camp session, re-create arts and crafts hour. These activities can be especially helpful if your camp gets rained out. Create friendship bracelets, make dream catchers, have a creative writing hour, and learn to bullet journal.

TRIVIA AND OTHER FREE GAMES

Host a '90s Nickelodeon Trivia Night with questions about characters, music introductions, names of hosts for game shows, series time lines, and more. Using multimedia for pictures, video, and sound will enhance your patrons' trivia experience even more.

MARKETING

- Re-create as much of the marketing and imagery from the game shows and TV shows as you like, as long as copyright permits.

- Hold the "Are You Afraid of the Dark?" program during Halloween for greater tie-ins to scary stories and bonfire nights, or plan the "Salute Your Shorts" program during the height of summer for a camp-like experience.

VARIATIONS BY AGE GROUPS

- *Tweens*: Make Nickelodeon slime. For instructions, see "How to Make Slime" on the Teen Vogue website (https://www.teenvogue.com/story/how-to-make-nickelodeon-slime).

- *Tweens*: Many tweens will not have the same nostalgic feelings attached to these programs that millennials have, but they will enjoy many of the wild and wacky challenges nonetheless.

- *Families*: Many of the Nickelodeon game show challenges can work for parent-and-child teams or for kids versus parents.

> **PRO TIP**
>
> **To familiarize yourself** with some of the Nickelodeon shows and learn the game show rules, search for clips on YouTube.

POP MUSIC: BOY BANDS AND GIRL POWER!

The '90s are often defined by the music of the era, and there was no better time for pop music. Boy bands and strong female artists dominated the music scene throughout the '90s. Relive the heyday of pop music, memorable music videos, iconic fashion statements, and girl power with creative programming that will attract millennials into the library.

PREP TIME	LENGTH OF PROGRAM	NUMBER OF PATRONS	SUGGESTED AGE RANGE
1½ hours	1 hour	20–30	Millennials

SUPPLIES/SHOPPING

Karaoke or Lip Sync
- Laptop
- Projector
- Screen
- '90s props (see suggestions in the activities section)

Music Video Remake
- Laptop
- Projector
- Screen
- DVD: MTV Behind the Scenes
- Portable green screen or backdrop of CD cover
- Props

'90s Hair
- Hair accessories
- Butterfly clips
- Rhinestone clips
- Multipack combs
- Small hair ties
- '90s fashion books
- Hair crimper

Girl Power
- Pogs
- Printed lyrics or song titles
- Mod Podge
- Blank paper
- Markers
- Resin (optional)
- Pin backings (optional)
- Button maker (optional)

ACTIVITIES

- *Karaoke or Lip Sync*: Host a karaoke or lip sync contest in which only '90s pop music can be played. This '90s music power hour can be complete with fun props, such as inflatable microphones, hats, beaded necklaces, and more. This program can be done as easily as setting up a laptop with YouTube lyric videos or adding closed captions and projecting them onto a screen.

- *Music Video Remake*: Bring in a dance instructor, or use old behind-the-scenes DVDs, and learn the choreography for some classic '90s music videos. Learning entire routines in an hour is unrealistic, but the chorus can be taught in a shorter time. Choose one or two classic music videos, such as *Bye Bye Bye* by *NSYNC or Destiny's Child's *Bills, Bills, Bills*. This is also a great time to relive an old episode of the MTV classic show *Making the Video*.

  Use a portable green screen or preprinted backdrop with props to re-create iconic CD covers, such as *NSYNC's *No Strings Attached* or the Spice Girls' *Spice* album. Patrons will enjoy the option of taking pictures with old favorites and reliving memories.

CRAFTS

'90s Hair
- Re-create some of the iconic fashions and hairstyles that adorned pop group members in the '90s. Bring out the butterfly clips, crimper, glitter gel, and colorful hair extensions. Print pictures of music celebrities from awards shows and music videos sporting these hair styles, and scavenge your collection for '90s fashion books. Consider partnering with a cosmetology school in your area, and take pictures for future '90s programs you want to promote.

Girl Power
- Have a creative session of girl-powered crafts by upcycling '90s pogs to make buttons paired with girl-powered '90s song titles and lyrics with pictures,

such as "Independent Woman," "Who Do You Think You Are," and "Just a Girl" by No Doubt. Print key lyrics or titles and provide markers and blank paper to encourage patrons to create their own lyrics and titles. Cut up the paper with the lyric or saying, Mod Podge it onto the pog, and glue on the pin backing This craft can also be done with a button maker or bottle caps, resin, and pin backings.

TRIVIA AND OTHER FREE GAMES

There are many options for '90s-themed music trivia: match the song lyrics to the boy or girl band, fill in the blank song lyrics, or identify key members in a band.

MARKETING

- On posters, use stylized images and graphics that look like the albums of '90s bands. Try an "I Love the '90s" text, similar to VH1's show, and, of course, have pictures of your favorite boy or girl singers.

- Place flyers near your CD collection or create a '90s CD display, if possible.

VARIATIONS BY AGE GROUPS

- *Tweens*: Many of these program ideas can be adapted for current pop music bands. Investigate online or at a tween program and see if there's a new popular band that is releasing an album soon. Have an album release party and stream the band's old and new music, have a trivia contest about song lyrics and band members, and create pins with pictures of the band's new album cover or members.

- *Older adults*: Create a music-themed program around iconic music of the '60s when the first waves of Top 40 and Classic Rock were coming to America, such as the Beatles and Rolling Stones. Play vinyl records and use scratched records to create vinyl-covered crafts, such as bookends or notebook covers.

PRO TIP

These activities can work well with the "I Want My MTV" program in the "1980s" chapter and the "Riot Grrrl Celebration" activities in this chapter.

RIOT GRRRL CELEBRATION: ZINE AND BUTTON MAKING

Riot grrrl was an underground punk movement that formed in the early '90s and inspired—and continues to inspire—feminists everywhere. Though a program featuring DIY pinback buttons and zines doesn't have to have a riot grrrl theme, there's also nothing that says it can't. Patrons of all ages will enjoy making crafts that allow them to express themselves, and those of a particular age will enjoy harking back to their younger, angstier days.

PREP TIME	LENGTH OF PROGRAM	NUMBER OF PATRONS	SUGGESTED AGE RANGE
2–3 hours	1 hour	25	Millennials

SUPPLIES/SHOPPING

- Button maker(s)
- Pinback button–making materials (shell, clear Mylar, collet, spring pin)
- Plain paper
- Construction paper
- Old or discarded magazines and newspapers
- Sharpies and pens
- Scissors
- Glue

ACTIVITIES

- *Zine Instructions*: The whole point of zines is that the content is entirely up to the creator, but patrons might need help with ways in which they can fold different sizes of paper to make different sizes of zines. For tips on ways to fold zines, refer to the Wikibooks page "Zine Making/Putting Pages Together" (http://bit.ly/2uq6ex8).

- In addition, consider throwing on a classic film like *Reality Bites* or *Empire Records* for patrons to enjoy while they craft (be sure to adjust the length of the program accordingly), or perhaps have early '90s grunge and riot grrrl classics on hand (Sleater-Kinney, Pearl Jam, Nirvana, etc.) to set the mood.

TRIVIA AND OTHER FREE GAMES

The riot grrrl movement occurred at a singular time in history that's rife with famous—and infamous—moments. Test participants' knowledge of the early to mid-'90s while they work on their creations.

MARKETING

- If your library has punk, grunge, and indie rock CDs (in addition to riot grrrl, of course), set up a music display with information about the program. Consider including early '90s fashions (think flannel, *lots* of flannel) as well!

- Get meta and make some quick zines that include information about the program.

VARIATIONS BY AGE GROUPS

It's not necessary to present this program in the guise of an angsty riot grrrl throwback because younger patrons may not have much, if any, riot grrrl nostalgia. Everyone can enjoy making buttons and zines! You can choose a different theme (or no theme at all) depending on the target audience.

2000s

As the century began in the year 2000, a few trends really stood out in food, movies, and television. This chapter looks at how entertainment changed in content and accessibility. Delicious "Cake Pops" start out the chapter with sweet bites that combine frosting and crumbled cake to make moldable treats. Get ready for messy fun with patrons as they explore this still-popular food trend. Comics and more can be celebrated at a "Collector Con," and this program details how to easily set one up. "Cult Movie Fest" and "Marvel Madness" look at genres, heroes, and icons as the library brings fandoms together. "Reality TV in Real Life" reminds audience members how entertainment changed completely with the advent of shows exploring . . . daily life. Participants in the "Revenge of the Nerds" program will see why science and fantasy are stylish in movies, TV shows, and books. Those genres inspired some of the most popular passions in this century so far, including Harry Potter and Lord of the Rings. And "TR-Not-So-L" adds crafts and group fun to karaoke to finish the timely genre programs.

CAKE POPS

With the popularity of the *Bakerella* blog and books, cake pops joined the mini baked goods craze in the early 2000s. Food reality shows such as *Cupcake Wars* and other themed baking competitions fueled interest. Making cake pops at the library can be messy, and they likely won't look like the cookbook versions, but that doesn't mean it isn't fun for you and audience members! Find simpler, fun ways to teach the basics of this fun food medium.

PREP TIME	LENGTH OF PROGRAM	NUMBER OF PATRONS	SUGGESTED AGE RANGE
4–5 hours, including baking and assembling of basic dough	1½ hours	20	Tweens, teens, millennials, older adults

SUPPLIES/SHOPPING

- Cake mix
- Frosting
- Candy melts (various colors)
- Lollipop sticks
- Styrofoam or holder for cake pops (for drying)
- Food markers
- Colored sprinkles
- Candies (small bits for decoration)
- Microwaves (at least 2)
- Microwave-safe bowls
- Waxed paper or parchment paper
- Paper plates (for cake pops to dry after dipping)
- Spoons (several)

ACTIVITIES

- Before the program, bake a cake mix in a 9-by-13-inch pan. When cooled, crumble the cake and mix it with ½ cup frosting, using your hands. Add only enough frosting to moisten the cake so the mixture will form balls (which will be made during the program). Chill overnight.

- When attendees arrive, invite them to sit in groups of four to five. Place a bowl of dough at each table, with plates lined with waxed paper or parchment paper in front of each chair. With clean hands, everyone should form small balls (1½ inches or so), or another shape, such as a football, insert a lollipop stick into each, and place them on the plate. Each group should choose a color for dipping and possibly another for accents. Melt the candy in bowls in the microwave and have each person at the table dip the cake pops into the melted candy. Either stand the pops up to dry or put them back on the plate (and remove the sticks). When the pops are dry, participants can decorate them using food markers or small bits of other candy and sprinkles.

TRIVIA AND OTHER FREE GAMES

- *Baking Trivia*: If the group has lots of willpower and can wait in between steps for the cake pops to dry before consuming, offer a baking utensil trivia challenge. Show photos of kitchen utensils and invite audience members to guess their uses.

- *School Spirit*: On football shapes, use sprinkles that are the colors for local teams.

MARKETING

Create a display of cake pops cookbooks and include photos or samples to attract people to the event.

VARIATIONS BY AGE GROUPS

- *Families: Design a Monster*—Offer more decorating candies and cereal bits and invite people to design monsters with the cake pops.

- *Older adults: Molded Cake Pops*—Show audience members how to line simple silicon candy or ice cube molds with the melted candy. After the candy has dried, participants can fill the molds with the dough before pouring more melted candy on top. Wait to dry again before carefully unmolding and eating or taking home.

> **PRO TIPS**
>
> **Make a few** samples before the program to get comfortable with the process.
>
> **The melted candy** hardens quickly, and some bowls may need to be microwaved again to keep the consistency liquid for dipping.

COLLECTOR CON

Collections come in all shapes and sizes, and holding a Collector Con at your library is a great opportunity to give the members of your community who have collections that they have amassed over years or even decades a chance to show them off.

PREP TIME	LENGTH OF PROGRAM	NUMBER OF PATRONS	SUGGESTED AGE RANGE
6–7 hours total, but you'll want to start several months before the planned date of your program in order to find participants	2–3 hours	Unlimited, depending on space	All ages

SUPPLIES/SHOPPING

- Tables
- Chairs
- Plenty of space!

ACTIVITIES

- *Program Planning*: Put out a call in your library's newsletter as well as online for local collectors who are interested in showing off some or all of their collections. Types of collections can include stamps, lunch boxes, dolls, action figures, souvenir spoons, shot glasses, magnets, and much, much more. You'll want to be sure, of course, that you look ahead at what space you are able to provide exhibitors and what you'll be able to provide in terms of tables and chairs. You will also want to be clear in stating that your library is not responsible for the safety of exhibitors' items, which people should take into account before signing up to participate. Have a letter of agreement that clearly states all the conditions and that will be signed by you and each exhibitor so that there is no confusion.

- *Program Setup*: All that is really required for this program is space for exhibitors to set up and show off their collections. Depending on what space(s) you're using for the program, consider creating a map or list of the exhibitors for attendees to refer to as they make their way around. You can include information about the exhibitors on the map or list as well, particularly if they have a blog or website about their collection.

MARKETING

- Reach out to local comics and collectibles shops for leads on artists and collectors in the area, and ask about posting flyers or program information in their establishments.

- Once the lineup of collectors is set, create a display of books about some of the collections that will be represented at the program, along with books about collecting and collectors' guides. Include information about the program on the display.

VARIATIONS BY AGE GROUPS

Variations aren't necessary, but it's a good idea to have a variety of collections represented to appeal to all ages.

CULT MOVIE FEST

What better way to celebrate pop culture than by indulging in some (family friendly) cult films from decades past? This program is very similar to the "Reboot Month" described in the "Pop Culture Review" chapter, but it differs by having more of a film festival feel, with a continuous showing of movies over the course of a day or a weekend.

PREP TIME	LENGTH OF PROGRAM	NUMBER OF PATRONS	SUGGESTED AGE RANGE
4–5 hours	Varies, depending on number of movies shown	Unlimited, depending on space	All ages (depending on movies selected)

SUPPLIES/SHOPPING

- Projection screen
- Digital projector
- DVD player
- Movie snacks and drinks (optional; popcorn, candy, fruit snacks, juice boxes, Capri Sun, soda, water)

ACTIVITIES

Family friendly cult classics include the following:

- *The Goonies* (PG)
- *Labyrinth* (PG)
- *The Princess Bride* (PG)
- *Ghostbusters* (PG; potential here for a crossover with the "Ghostbusted" program in the "1980s" chapter)
- *E.T. the Extra Terrestrial* (PG)
- *The Iron Giant* (PG)
- *Homeward Bound* (G)

TRIVIA AND OTHER FREE GAMES

Although you likely won't have time to play trivia during your movie fest, consider printing out sheets of information, including trivia, about each movie being shown and make the sheets available to patrons. Or, if you are showing two movies on one day but have planned break time between each viewing (recommended), you can play a few rounds of trivia during that time.

MARKETING

Create a display of the movies that you'll be featuring for the fest and include on it information about the program. Also include any additional materials (books, soundtracks, video games) related to the franchises that you'll be featuring.

VARIATIONS BY AGE GROUPS

Because this program is intended to be a showing of family friendly films, no variations are necessary!

MARVEL MADNESS

Though movies featuring superheroes have existed for several decades, the dawn of the new millennium brought a box office takeover by silver screen superheroes. No matter which hero or corner of the Marvel Universe you want to tackle, there are plenty of programming options.

PREP TIME	LENGTH OF PROGRAM	NUMBER OF PATRONS	SUGGESTED AGE RANGE
3–4 hours	1½–2 hours (or longer, depending on movie showings)	Unlimited, depending on space	All ages

SUPPLIES/SHOPPING

Buttons
- Button maker(s)
- Pinback button–making materials (shell, clear Mylar, collet, spring pin)
- Plain paper
- Markers, crayons, colored pencils
- Marvel stickers

Zines
- Plain paper
- Markers, crayons, colored pencils
- Old or discarded issues of Marvel comics
- Glue sticks
- Scissors
- Marvel stickers

Perler Beads
- Perler beads in a wide variety of colors
- Iron
- Marvel Perler bead patterns (available online)
- Pegboards (clear)
- Parchment paper

ACTIVITIES

- Obviously a great place to start is by showing a movie from the Marvel cinematic universe and pairing it with a low-key craft that patrons can complete while viewing. Detailed craft options are listed in the crafts section, but ones that work particularly well while viewing a film are zines and coloring sheets, particularly sheets featuring comics or blank panels so that patrons can create their own comics.

- *Crossover with Collector Con*: Chances are someone participating in the Collector Con will have a collection of comics or comic book memorabilia, so this is a great opportunity to invite that person to give a presentation about the items and to share knowledge of the subject.

- Explore options for partnering with a local comics shop for this program.

- *Book Discussion*: There are plenty of options for holding a book discussion in conjunction with a Marvel-centered program. Participants can discuss a particular graphic novel or a work of nonfiction about the Marvel company or about the people associated with it. Good options are *Marvel Comics: The Untold Story* by Sean Howe or *Amazing Fantastic Incredible: A Marvelous Memoir* by Stan Lee and Peter David.

CRAFTS

Zines

- Invite attendees to make their own comics and zines! If your library regularly has old or withdrawn copies of any of the numerous Marvel comics, set them out with zine-making supplies and encourage participants to make their own Marvel stories by cutting and pasting. For tips on different ways to fold zines, refer to the Wikibooks page "Zine Making/Putting Pages Together" (http://bit .ly/2uq6ex8).

Buttons

- Set out button-making supplies so that attendees can create a wearable way to show their love of Marvel! Include Marvel stickers with the supplies in addition to paper and coloring implements.

Perler Bead Heroes

- Marvel Perler bead patterns can be found online, and detailed information about working with Perler beads can be found on wikiHow (www.wikihow .com/Use-Perler-Beads).

TRIVIA AND OTHER FREE GAMES

Trivia abound about the Marvel Universe, both cinematic and print. You could, in fact, have an entire trivia night or round of your regular trivia night (if you have one) dedicated to Marvel trivia as a lead-up or promotional event for your library Comic Con (if you have one).

MARKETING

Create a display of Marvel movies and graphic novels, and include on it information about the program. Place the display near your graphic novel section(s) or near the AV section.

VARIATIONS BY AGE GROUPS

- *Millennials, older adults*: Consider crossing this program over with the "Holy Primetime, Batman! Superheroes on TV" program in the "1960s" chapter. Show an episode of *The Incredible Hulk* followed by clips or the entirety of one of the recent Hulk films.

- *Tweens, teens, older adults*: Hold multiple book or comics discussions based on age group. Tweens and teens might be more interested in a graphic novel discussion, whereas older adults might gravitate to a discussion of one of the nonfiction books mentioned in the activities section.

PRO TIP

The Marvel Universe contains heroes of all shapes, colors, sizes, and genders. Strive to be as inclusive as possible with your program!

REALITY TV IN REAL LIFE

The early 2000s brought a new wave of television to American homes: reality TV that pushed the boundaries and opened up a new era in primetime. Three shows emerged as "must-see television" as viewers tuned in to see how far contestants were willing to go to win. *Fear Factor, The Amazing Race,* and *Survivor* consisted of physical and mental challenges to test contestants' endurance. Modify popular challenges and games from these hit shows for a night of friendly (or fierce) competition at the library.

PREP TIME	LENGTH OF PROGRAM	NUMBER OF PATRONS	SUGGESTED AGE RANGE
4 hours	1 hour	20–30	Teens

SUPPLIES/SHOPPING ·······························

Fear Factor
- Paper plates
- Paper bowls
- Paper cups
- Food and drink choices for challenges (see suggestions in the activities section)
- Bottled water
- Whiteboard
- Dry-erase markers

Amazing Library Race
- Paper
- Pens or pencils
- Timer
- Scavenger hunt clues
- Water guns (optional)

Survivor
- Minute to Win It game supplies (see suggestions in the activities section)
- Tropical island decor (beach balls, tiki torches, inflatable palm tree props, etc.)
- Tropical fruit assortment
- Timer
- Whiteboard
- Dry-erase markers

ACTIVITIES ··

- *Fear Factor:* Challenge teens to consume different foods or drinks (be sure to ask patrons if they have any food allergies before beginning the program). Foods and drinks can range from mild and innocuous to spicy and extreme (for example, prune juice, pickled eggs, Wasabi peas, Flaming Hot Cheetos, green baby food, and chocolate-covered crickets). Rank each food or drink with a point system, so if teens decide not to try one item or are allergic, they can still gain points by trying others. Unique foods, such as chocolate-covered crickets, get more points, and the person or team with the most points at the end wins! Keep track of team scores on a whiteboard or paper, and have bottled water on hand for contestants.

- *Amazing Library Race*: Create an Amazing Library Race! Patrons sign up in teams or create teams on the spot to discover hidden caches and information in the library by uncovering riddles and clues. Hide clues in stacks, different areas of the library, and outside if your library has a safe walking area or town square. This can be a scavenger hunt of sorts or a mission to solve clues that relate specifically to your library.

  Create checkpoints in the race for teams to find library staff members or volunteers to do a silly task, such as forming a kick line or doing jumping jacks, to earn a signature for a point. If teams are going outside, teen volunteers can act as enforcers to make sure participants are safely crossing streets and not running; provide water guns to the enforcers to squirt offending teams. Have each team start the race on a different question so teams are not running into each other, and the team that has the most correct points when everyone is due back in the room wins.

- *Survivor*: Transform your program room into a *Survivor* island. Decorate the room with a tropical or island theme and provide a tropical fruit assortment to create an island atmosphere.

  Teens can register for the program in tribes (aka teams), or you can place them in tribes when the program begins. The tribe that wins each Minute to Win It game gets immunity for that round and cannot be eliminated. Instead of having tribes vote each other off the island, tribe names are put into a drawing to be eliminated. Eliminated tribes can assist with other challenges to keep everyone involved in the program. At the end of the games, the winner is the tribe left standing or the team that has won the most games.

  Change Minute to Win It games to be more *Survivor*-like, such as the following.

  » *Injured Teammate Mummy Wrap*: Use a toilet paper roll to wrap a teammate's wound. The tribe that does this fastest wins.
  » *Gone Fishing*: Hide Swedish Fish in a baby pool or sensory table filled with sand and whipped cream. Each team sends one teammate at a time to get as many fish as possible in one minute. Change this challenge by blindfolding the teens hunting for the fish or by putting in only one fish for everyone to find.

» *Beach Ball Boulders*: Each teammate in a tribe has to blow a beach ball from one end of the room to the other using a straw.

» *Water Challenge*: Teams have to fill a milk carton with water using a plastic cup that can only be passed from teammate to teammate using their feet.

MARKETING

- When creating promotional posters, use stylized logos similar to those from the reality shows you will be replicating.

- Create a display for your program with books that highlight courage, daring exploits, and survival. Include biographies. Print *Survivor*-style banners and use a tropical grass skirt to cover the table. Include flyers advertising the program in the display.

- *Fear Factor* has a built-in marketing appeal for the month of October. Plan your program around Halloween or Friday the 13th, if possible.

VARIATIONS BY AGE GROUPS

- *All ages*: The Amazing Library Race can be done as a passive program over a span of time with paper and pen, online, or by geocaching (setting coordinates in specific locations and hiding containers for patrons to find using GPS and smartphones).

- *All ages*: For a less competitive programming approach, plan an *America's Got Talent* night at your library. Name the program after your own library (for example, "Schaumburg Township District Library's Got Talent") and open up the competition for a special one-time talent show. Participants will have an opportunity to show off their unique skills in front of family, friends, and library patrons, and you will have a chance to learn about your community members.

- *Millennials, older adults*: Bring in a National Park Service ranger or survival expert to speak about living off the land and orienteering. Many will find this reminiscent of Bear Grylls's *Man vs. Wild* television series.

PRO TIPS

Check with library management if you are doing a particularly risky challenge. A waiver or special permission may be needed.

If you have groups of teens moving in teams around the library or outside on a particular night, notify departments and desk staff ahead of time.

REVENGE OF THE NERDS

Nerds shall inherit the earth! The 2000s saw a conscious shift in the pop culture world in which being a nerd no longer meant being weird or ostracized from peers for seemingly nerdy interests. The rise of the Internet gave people the chance to connect online and organize in person at meetups and large-scale conventions, such as Comic Con. Pop culture nerd stereotypes became mainstream with relatable media characters, TV shows, and movies, such as the *Lord of the Rings* movies, *The Big Bang Theory,* the Harry Potter movies, and the rise of comic book superhero movies. The words *nerd* and *geek* were reappropriated from something to be ashamed of to becoming synonymous with being progressive or passionate about an interest. Give patrons the opportunity to own their nerdom and geek out among their peers, either in a single fandom or nerd-based program or a series.

PREP TIME	LENGTH OF PROGRAM	NUMBER OF PATRONS	SUGGESTED AGE RANGE
2 hours	1 hour	10–20	Teens

SUPPLIES/SHOPPING

Nerd Snacks
- Smarties
- Nerds
- Fruit punch
- Jelly beans (for Bertie Bott's Every Flavour Beans)
- Graham crackers
- Marshmallows
- Pretzel rods
- Chocolate melts (various colors)
- Labels (to indicate the foods and associated fandoms)
- Cups
- Plates
- Napkins

Nerdfighters
- Computer
- Projector and screen

Fan Fiction Mashup
- Pencils or pens
- Paper

Book Discussion
- Book or graphic novel of choice

Fandom Perler Beads
- Perler beads
- Perler bead boards
- Waxed paper
- Iron
- Glue
- Magnets

Nerd Tote Bag
- Canvas tote bags
- Acrylic paint
- Paintbrushes
- Cups (for water)

ACTIVITIES

- *Nerd Snacks*: Theme up your nerd party snacks with Nerds, Smarties, Princess Peach punch, and Bertie Bott's Every Flavour Beans. Teens can create (and eat) TIE Fighters using graham crackers and marshmallows. Set up a chocolate dipping station for teens to create lightsaber pretzel rods.

- *Nerdfighters*: Show a video or two from John and Hank Green's Nerdfighters YouTube channel and let teens get informed about the world around them, pop culture and current events, and the amazing power of Nerdfighters. DFTBA—Don't Forget to Be Awesome!

- *Geek Out*: Participants can share their nerdery and fandom obsessions with the group. Teens will have one minute each to share their favorite fandom, explaining what it is about, why it's their favorite, and how they got involved with it. This is a great icebreaker and an opportunity to find like-minded peers who share common interests and to bond over characters. It's also a chance to find new fandoms and interests based on recommendations from other self-proclaimed nerds. This activity can also be a great way to discover patrons' fandom interests and how to cultivate future programs.

- *Fan Fiction Mashup*: Do creative writing exercises in which patrons must incorporate different characters or settings from at least two fandoms. These stories can be funny, startling, sad, or whatever the writer chooses and will encourage teens to think about how characters from different universes will react when meeting or crossing over into another's world. Use prompts such as two people meeting at a parent-teacher conference, one character suddenly falling into the other's world, two people waiting in line at a carnival, and so on. To shake things up even more, write the names of different fandoms, protagonists, or antagonists on slips of paper and have teens draw them randomly from a box to include them in their story. Stories can be as long or short as desired.

- *Book Discussion*: If you choose to focus on and celebrate a particular fandom or theme, ask attendees to read a book or graphic novel in advance for a book discussion. For example, pair a Wonder Woman fandom party with *Wonder*

Woman: Warbringer by Leigh Bardugo. Another way to include attendees is to ask everyone to bring in their favorite Avengers graphic novel to share favorite story lines, quotes, and more.

CRAFTS

Fandom Perler Beads

- Make unique fandom designs out of Perler beads. Show off nerdy interests in the form of a Perler bead design, whether it is a superhero logo, a Star Wars droid, a book cover, or a video game character. Iron with a waxed paper sheet on top to solidify and glue a magnet onto the back, if desired.

Nerd Tote Bag

- Teens can create personalized book tote bags that proclaim their nerdom with the words *Book Geek, Nerd,* or *Book Nerd* and a fandom logo, eyeglasses, or a book icon. This can be done by silk screening or using traditional acrylic paint and paintbrushes. If the program is fandom specific, attendees can use phrases and icons from that fandom. As a bonus, this program will give patrons something to carry their library books in.

TRIVIA AND OTHER FREE GAMES

- Teens can play charades and act out different fandoms for their teammates or select particular scenes if the program is fandom specific.

- Play music from specific movies and TV shows and have attendees guess the names.

- Trivia for many specific fandoms is endless—patrons will eagerly play.

MARKETING

- Use stereotypical images such as eyeglasses or books and the word *nerd* to promote this program.

- Create a book display of popular fandom titles to promote the program. Ask your patrons, "What do you geek?" and create an interactive element to the display, if possible.

- Many of the suggested fandom activities would be great as lead-up programs to a library Comic Con event or during the event.

VARIATIONS BY AGE GROUPS ·····························

- *All ages*: Create a fan art contest that will run for a month or another set time. This gives patrons the opportunity to build their work over a longer period of time.

- *Tweens*: Have a mad scientist lab and re-create some YouTube science experiments, such as the following:

  » *Lava Lamp Science*: Combine water, oil, food coloring, and an Alka Seltzer tablet to create a lava lamp effect in a cup or jar (see http://on.mash .to/2ukaOxW).
  » *Elephant Toothpaste*: Combine hydrogen peroxide, food coloring, and a few drops of dish soap in a bottle. Add yeast and warm water to a smaller cup and mix together. Add the yeast mixture to the bottle, which should cause a small exothermic foam reaction that will overflow (see https:// www.wikihow.com/Make-Elephant-Toothpaste).
  » *Egg Walk*: Walk barefoot on eggs in the cardboard egg carton. The mass distribution over the eggs should cause the eggs to remain intact.

- *Millennials*: Show an old episode of *Freaks and Geeks* in which the nerds were outcasts. Show clips of life in the '90s with nerdom on the periphery. Have a LAN party and get everyone connected to play multiplayer video games for hours on end. Other possibilities can include classic video or board games, such as Risk or Nintendo 64. Don't forget the junk food!

- *All ages*: Remember your elementary school photos or your family's Sears portraits? Re-create an iconic family photo twenty years later at the library by providing a green screen background. Ask patrons to call ahead and set up five- to ten-minute time slots and to bring their own flash drive.

PRO TIP

Get inspired by your collection and use these books as reference guides: *The Fangirl's Guide to the Galaxy* by Sam Maggs and *The Fangirl Life* by Kathleen Smith.

TR-NOT-SO-L

Who doesn't remember racing home from school, grabbing a package of Gushers, and plopping down in front of the TV to watch Carson Daly count down that day's top ten music videos on MTV? Those were simpler days, but the magic can be recaptured if only for one brief evening. Take your patrons on a trip back to the early 2000s with this fun and easy karaoke program.

PREP TIME	LENGTH OF PROGRAM	NUMBER OF PATRONS	SUGGESTED AGE RANGE
2–3 hours	1–1½ hours	20–25	Millennials

SUPPLIES/SHOPPING

- Karaoke machine
- TV
- Karaoke versions of late '90s and early 2000s hits

Cassette Tape Pencil Holder (optional)
- Cassettes (4 per holder; can be found for very little money at thrift stores—stock up so you've got plenty for patrons to choose from)
- Sharp knife
- Glue gun
- Cardboard
- Scissors

ACTIVITIES

Karaoke is fairly self-explanatory. Decide whether to allow patrons to choose the songs they want to perform or whether the songs will be chosen by you, at random, or by a vote (in homage to the top ten nature of TRL). Wikipedia has a page collecting all the videos that held the number one spot throughout the show's entire ten-year run (http://bit.ly/2u0uTIC), so another option is to look at the videos that were popular during a particular year around the same month and day of your program and use those to create a karaoke playlist.

CRAFTS

Cassette Tape Pencil Holder

- True, most of us had moved on to CDs by the time TRL came around, but some diehards cling to their beloved "As Long as You Love Me" cassingle to this very day. Show your patrons a fun way to display their love of nostalgia by creating a cassette tape pencil holder. For instructions, see the "I Want My MTV" program in the "1980s" chapter or visit Upcycle That (https://www.upcyclethat.com/upcycled-cassettes/2297/).

TRIVIA AND OTHER FREE GAMES

While you're testing people's memories of the lyrics of popular songs from the late '90s and 2000s, why not also test their knowledge of the major events, fads, and entertainment of that period?

MARKETING

Create a CD display of the major players from the TRL days—Backstreet Boys, Britney Spears, Christina Aguilera, *NSYNC, Usher, and the like—and include on it information about the program.

VARIATIONS BY AGE GROUPS

Switch up the music choices based on the particular age group you're targeting. For example, today's tweens and teens might be more interested in singing current songs, whereas millennials and older adults might be happier with '80s and early '90s karaoke. But everyone loves a good cassette tape pencil holder!

> **PRO TIP**
>
> **No karaoke machine?** No problem! Depending on your library's music collection, snag some CDs to use, throw them into a laptop, look up lyrics on a site such as lyrics.com, if necessary, and you're good to go. For fewer CDs but plenty of options, look for any volumes of *Now That's What I Call Music!*—arguably the greatest anthology series of ultra-popular pop hits.

Pop Culture Review

This final chapter features programs that look at trends across decades—food, fashions, movies, even cars. "Classic Candies by the Decade" will remind patrons why some delectable sweets have been around for one hundred years or more. "Classic Cars" offers activities inside and outside the library for all ages to appreciate. "Decades of Disney" will no doubt also be popular for patrons of all ages to experience. "Fashion Trendsetters" looks at what made style trendsetters famous, from Audrey Hepburn to Kate Middleton. Patrons will enjoy remembering, playing, and competing in "Games" from several decades. Star Wars and Star Trek are two of the "Popular Franchises" that keep returning to entertainment and culture, and more will be seen in "Reboot Month." Completing the review is a celebration of food and music in "Treats and Beats by the Decade."

CLASSIC CANDIES BY THE DECADE

Similar in style to the "Treats and Beats by the Decade" program also in this chapter, "Classic Candies by the Decade" offers sweet samples by era.

PREP TIME	LENGTH OF PROGRAM	NUMBER OF PATRONS	SUGGESTED AGE RANGE
1½ hours	1½ hours	35	Tweens, teens, older adults, families

SUPPLIES/SHOPPING

- For ideas about what to serve for each decade, see CandyFavorites.com (https://www.candyfavorites.com/shop/history-american-candy.php).
- Plates
- Napkins
- Water
- Cups

ACTIVITIES

- Introduce each decade and give a few facts and history of each point in time. Be sure to offer any candies that are locally made or have regional connections. Mention a few facts about each candy.

- Be sure to discuss some candies that are no longer made and ask participants about their favorites and memories of particular candies, especially with an audience that has lots of senior citizens.

- Consider hosting this event more than once for different age groups.

- Many candies are available from each decade, but here are some suggestions:
  - » 1940s: M&M's, Junior Mints, Smarties
  - » 1950s: Marshmallow Peeps, Pixy Stix
  - » 1960s: Starburst Fruit Chews, 100 Grand bars, Cadbury Creme Eggs
  - » 1970s: Snickers, Twix, Jelly Bellys
  - » 1980s: Gummy bears, Skittles, Symphony bars
  - » 1990s: Dove chocolates

TRIVIA AND OTHER FREE GAMES

Match the Slogan to the Candy: Using popular slogans for each candy, see if people can match the advertising to the item.

MARKETING

Make bookmarks that look like candy wrappers with the program information to hand out at the circulation desk prior to the event.

VARIATIONS

- *Holiday Candies by the Decade*: Offer treats that were introduced from 1950 on. This program could also be offered at Valentine's Day.

- *Chocolate by the Decade*: This program could also feature cakes or hot chocolate variations and voting.

CLASSIC CARS

All ages will enjoy car activities with these interactive events—inside and outside the library.

PREP TIME	LENGTH OF PROGRAM	NUMBER OF PATRONS	SUGGESTED AGE RANGE
2 hours (more for the vintage car show for registration, organization)	1½ hours for most activities inside the library	30 for toy car games and edible cars, more for the vintage car show, movie fest, and collecting presentation	Older adults, families

SUPPLIES/SHOPPING

Hot Wheels Track Racing
- Hot Wheels Versus Track Set for tabletop racing, or track sets
- Hot Wheels cars (assorted)
- *Optional*: Set up an incline with books and use for racing (participants can also design their own racing tracks)

Edible Cars
- Paper plates
- Plastic knives
- Rice Krispies Treats
- Pop-Tarts
- Frosting (in cans)
- Round cookies
- Gumdrops
- Licorice

ACTIVITIES

- *Vintage Car Show*: Invite patrons who own vintage cars to display them in a designated section of the parking lot. Participants will need to register and agree to stay with their vehicles. The library could provide drinks and snacks.

- *Cars-by-the-Decade Photo Contest*: Place a time line on a bulletin board and post pictures submitted by patrons of their cars in decades past.

- *Car Movie Fest*: In the weeks before the event, have patrons vote for their favorite car-themed movies or movies with chase scenes. Show the winners in a series or in a single day.

- *Toy Car Collecting*: Invite a toy collector to discuss brands and value. Or invite local collectors to display their collections at tables and talk with people who come to look at the items.

- *Track for Remote Control Cars*: Build an outdoor area for remote control cars. Invite patrons to bring their own cars. Have volunteers or teen helpers design a library-themed course. This activity could be done indoors as well, but space is needed.

- *Hot Wheels Track Racing*: Set up an area for Hot Wheels racing, either with a library-made incline or a purchased set.

CRAFTS

Edible Cars
- Invite young people or families to build edible cars from the food and candy elements available.

MARKETING

The time line of car photos and voting for the movie fest will help advertise this program.

VARIATIONS BY AGE GROUPS

Teens, millennials: Car Care 101—Ask employees of a local garage to demonstrate oil checking and tire changing in a section of the parking lot. Winter weatherizing is another good topic.

DECADES OF DISNEY

The world of Walt Disney has had fans of all ages throughout the world ever since Mickey Mouse appeared on the screen in 1928. More than just princesses, Disney has the unique ability to prompt discussion and connect people throughout the generations through animation. Choose from the many activities and crafts that correlate to the age group you want to target for your Disney-based program.

PREP TIME	LENGTH OF PROGRAM	NUMBER OF PATRONS	SUGGESTED AGE RANGE
3–4 hours	1–3 hours (depending on movies shown)	20–30	All ages

SUPPLIES/SHOPPING

Disney Book to Movie
- Disney movie of choice
- Fairy-tale books made into Disney movies
- Disney-themed snacks

Costume Sing-Along
- Disney Sing-Along DVD or DVD with closed captions
- Projector and screen

Disney Movie Roast
- Laptop
- MuVChat app
- Projector and screen
- Disney movie of choice

Disney Peep Art Dioramas
- Peeps
- Shoeboxes
- Embellishments
- Sharpies or markers
- Construction paper
- Glue

DIY Disney Hacked Dresses
- Sewing needles
- Sewing machines (if available, but not necessary)
- Thread
- Scissors
- Fabric of choice

Disney Accessories
- Mickey or Minnie Mouse Headband
  » Fabric headbands
  » Foam core boards
  » Scissors
  » Hot glue guns and glue sticks
  » Colored or patterned fabric
  » Ribbon

- Ursula Seashell Necklace
  » Black cord
  » Seashells
  » Yellow paint
  » Glitter
  » Paintbrushes
  » Cup with water for brushes

- Snow White Apple
  » Plastic red apples
  » Green fabric paint
  » Elmer's glue
  » Cup to mix water and glue
  » Paintbrushes

ACTIVITIES

- *Disney Book to Movie*: For a book discussion group, read a classic fairy tale that was made into a Disney movie and show the accompanying movie or short film. This activity can be part of an existing program series or a stand-alone program. Following the movie, have a discussion comparing the book to its movie incarnation. If you do this as a series, discuss how Disney movies have changed over the years. How do they compare or hold up in today's modern society? Are the subjects historically accurate and represented in a culturally sensitive way?

- *Costume Sing-Along*: Host a costume parade and sing-along night for a popular Disney movie. Some popular Disney DVDs have sing-along versions or add closed captions to a traditional Disney DVD. Have a fashion show and parade through the children's section so kids can show off their costumes before or after the movie. Encourage staff members to wear costumes for greater buy-in.

- *Disney Movie Roast*: Is Disney too sweet and saccharine for your teens? Have a snark fest and roast a Disney movie of choice. Download the MuVChat app on library iPads or on teens' smartphones for a small fee to let patrons chime in on-screen through the app, and let the snarky comments begin!

CRATS ···

Disney Peep Art Dioramas

- Re-create classic Disney scenes in Peep dioramas. Patrons can decorate and strategically arrange Peeps in a shoebox or homemade diorama. Use Sharpies or markers to decorate the Peep Disney characters and background. Create a display with the finished products.

DIY Disney Hacked Dresses

- Hack an ordinary dress into a Disney-themed dress based on popular Disney characters or princesses. This activity could draw in high school students attending a school dance or adults going to a wedding. Starting with an existing dress, add an Elsa cape, stitch on polka dots to make a Minnie Mouse dress, or use colored tulle in the Disney princess colors of your choice. Pair this activity with a fashion program and use sewing machines if your library has them, but they are not necessary. Consider collaborating with high schools or local colleges that have classes or offer degrees in fashion. Another option is to have participants design their own dresses based on Disney characters, but this will require a much longer program or a series.

DISNEY ACCESSORIES ···

Create a crafting program involving Disney accessories. Crafting possibilities can include the following:

- *Mickey or Minnie Mouse Headband:* Cut out four Mickey Mouse–shaped ears from foam core, two for each side to add depth. Using the hot glue gun, glue both sides of each ear together and then glue colored or patterned fabric to both sides of the ears. Add a ribbon to the sides to cover up any seams, and glue ears to a fabric headband. Add a bow in the middle to make a Minnie Mouse headband.

- *Ursula Seashell Necklace:* Paint a circular seashell yellow and add glitter on top, if desired. Glue black cord onto the shell and add a knot at the end to make a necklace.

- *Snow White Apple:* Outline the eyes and mouth of the Snow White skull apple in green fabric paint on a plastic red apple. Combine small amounts of water and white glue in a cup with the green fabric paint and paint the mixture on the top, letting it slowly drip down the sides. Let dry completely (overnight).

TRIVIA AND OTHER FREE GAMES

- Disney trivia is a must for any Disney movie buff. Questions can range from the inception of Mickey Mouse and Steamboat Willie to Disneyland facts and current movies.

- *BYOG (Bring Your Own Game):* Ask patrons to bring their favorite Disney-themed board games to play and share with others. Serve Disney-themed snacks and treats found at your local grocery store.

MARKETING

- Disney is always prolific and popular, no matter the time of year, but if a Disney movie is being released or remade, choose a craft or activity to promote and coincide with it for extra relevancy.

- Depending on your targeted age group, displaying Disney books isn't always the right choice because most tend to skew younger. Use princess-themed colors and iconic imagery, such as yellow and roses for *Beauty and the Beast* or light blue and snowflakes for *Frozen.* If you have finished examples of the crafts, display them in a 3-D case, if possible.

VARIATIONS BY AGE GROUPS

Choose activities and crafts that are appropriate for your targeted age group, but many can apply to varying age groups.

PRO TIP

This program has crossover potential with "Reboot Month" with a Disney theme. Show the animated and live-action versions or show a collection of the shorts and pair them with a suggested activity.

FASHION TRENDSETTERS

Enjoy this fashionable trip back through the decades by looking at style icons. This program can be purely informative or have a fashion accessory craft component.

PREP TIME	LENGTH OF PROGRAM	NUMBER OF PATRONS	SUGGESTED AGE RANGE
2 hours	1½ hours (longer with craft)	50, or 25 with craft	Teens, millennials, older adults

SUPPLIES/SHOPPING

Pendant Necklaces
- Antique gold necklace chains (available in bulk from Amazon)
- Antique gold bezel pendant blanks, round
- Scrapbook paper, cut into 1-inch circles (2 per participant)
- Assorted small beads, charms
- Sun and Moon Glaze or Diamond Glaze
- E-6000 glue

ACTIVITIES

Show photos of style icons from each decade, especially items that could be copied today. Pinterest has guides to dressing like many of these icons with modern clothes.

1950s
- Audrey Hepburn (www.vintag.es/2015/04/beautiful-fashions-of-audrey-hepburn-in.html)
- Discuss cigarette pants, striped tops, black sheath dresses.
- Poodle skirts (see also the "'50s Chic" program in the "1950s" chapter)
- Grace Kelly (https://www.liveabout.com/dress-like-an-icon-grace-kelly-3419875)
- Show examples of circle skirts, structured handbags, white shirts.

1960s
- Jackie O (her photos could cover several decades: www.instyle.com/fashion/jackie-kennedy-style-lessons#1317896)
- The hat and suit sets with boxy jackets were a signature look.

- Twiggy (http://womens-fashion.lovetoknow.com/Twiggy_Fashion_1960s)
- Miniskirts and high boots are memorable from this time.

1970s

- Wrap dresses (www.marieclaire.co.uk/fashion/the-story-of-diane-von
-furstenberg-s-most-iconic-dresses-30763)
- Iman (https://www.vogue.com/article/fashion-beauty-iman-supermodel
-models-diversity-yves-saint-laurent)
- Bell-bottoms, long tunic tops, halter dresses (www.marieclaire.co.uk/
fashion/1970s-fashion-moments-that-defined-seventies-style-96107)

1980s

- Madonna (www.billboard.com/photos/428558madonnas-most-iconic
-looks-throughout-the-years)
- Fingerless gloves, hair bows, layered off-the-shoulder looks

1990s

- Princess Diana ('80s and '90s; www.instyle.com/celebrity/princess-dianas
-most-iconic-style-moments#250741)
- Discuss the outfits Princess Di wore that audience members remember.
- Western wear, flannel, layered skirts with slips showing underneath, con-
trasting visible lingerie straps

1990s–2000s

- Discuss trends that audience members enjoyed and currently wear.
- Jennifer Lopez (www.billboard.com/photos/428535/jennifer-lopez-style
-evolution)
- Lady Gaga (www.vogue.co.uk/gallery/style-file-lady-gaga)
- Compare with Cher (www.billboard.com/photos/5719494/chers-25-most
-outrageous-outfits)
- Kim Kardashian (www.glamourmagazine.co.uk/gallery/kim-kardashian
-new-style-high-fashion-wardrobe)
- Discuss the "street style" that KK exhibits.
- Lupita Nyong'o (www.harpersbazaar.com/celebrity/red-carpet-dresses/
g7882/lupita-nyongos-best-looks/)
- Discuss makeup, bold color choices.
- Michelle Obama (https://www.nytimes.com/2017/01/14/fashion/
michelle-obama-first-lady-fashion.html)
- Trends from Michelle Obama: sleeveless or one-shouldered gowns, fitted
outfits, J. Crew
- Beyoncé (www.elle.com/fashion/celebrity-style/news/g7684beyonce
-best-fashion-looks/)

- Compare with Lady Gaga, Cher, Madonna
- Kate Middleton (www.harpersbazaar.com/fashion/trends/g1811/kate-middleton-outfits/)
- Compare with Princess Diana
- Also for modern times, discuss the current interest in steampunk and pendant necklaces.

CRAFTS

Pendant Necklaces

- A more elaborate version of this craft is featured on the *BlueKatKraft* blog (http://blukatkraft.blogspot.com/2012/01/easy-diy-vintage-collage-pendants.html).

- Before the presentation, have participants glue first one scrapbook paper circle and then another into the bezel pendant shells. Start the presentation. Take a break after about fifteen minutes. Have attendees glue a few small beads and one charm onto their necklaces. Allow to dry while the presentation continues for another fifteen to twenty minutes. Crafters then fill in around the glued objects with Diamond or Sun and Moon Glaze. Participants will need to carefully take their pendants home so they can dry overnight.

TRIVIA AND OTHER FREE GAMES

Match the Era to the Item: Show examples of accessories or dresses from each decade and see if people can match the items to the correct decade.

MARKETING

- Displays of fashion items from past decades would be fun if available from staff. Include information about the program on the display.

- Posters with information about the program will also attract attention.

PRO TIP

Make a sample of the pendant necklace before the event to get the timing down for each step.

GAMES

No matter the era in question, it's not difficult to find the most popular games of that time. There are several ways to approach planning programs that celebrate gaming throughout pop culture history, and here we have provided a few suggestions for how you can go about it.

PREP TIME	LENGTH OF PROGRAM	NUMBER OF PATRONS	SUGGESTED AGE RANGE
3–4 hours	3 hours	Unlimited (done as a drop-in program)	All ages

SUPPLIES/SHOPPING

In addition to the games themselves, it's not a bad idea to have extra paper and pencils on hand for the games that require score keeping.

Life-Size Gaming
- Foam squares
- Balloons
- Decorations (inflatable dice, character cutouts, large spinners, playing cards, etc., all from popular games to set the tone of the day)

Board Game 3-D Design
- 3-D printer
- 3-D scanner or Xbox Kinect
- Foam core board
- Pens, pencils

Bookmarks
- Game boards
- X-acto knife or box cutter
- Hole punch
- Ribbon

Coasters
- Game boards
- Glue (something quick drying like E-6000)
- Scrabble tiles
- Cork (optional)

Ornaments
- Glue (something quick drying like E-6000)
- Scrabble tiles and holders
- Screw eye hooks
- Ribbon

Decoupage Notebook Covers
- Mod Podge or decoupage glue
- Small notebooks
- Paper pieces from board games

ACTIVITIES ···

Games by the Decade: Create a series of programs in which each installment celebrates the popular games of a particular decade. Each program can be held as a drop-in, so patrons don't need to arrive at a particular start time but can drop in any time to play for whatever amount of time they choose.

Game suggestions by decade:

- 1950s: Dominoes, Checkers, Yahtzee, Chutes and Ladders, Candyland, Clue, Scrabble
- 1960s: Stratego, Trouble, Operation, KerPlunk, Battleship, Twister, Mystery Date
- 1970s: Hungry Hungry Hippos, Connect Four, Stratego
- 1980s: Trivial Pursuit, Balderdash, Labyrinth, Mall Madness, Girl Talk
- 1990s: Where in the World Is Carmen Sandiego?, Jumanji, Dream Phone
- 2000s: Scene It?, Ticket to Ride, Pandemic
  - » You can find many of these games at secondhand or thrift stores. Ask coworkers if they have any of these games that they would be willing to let the library use for the day or if they have any other classic games from the specific decade.

- *Life-Size Gaming:* Create a life-size game out of one or more of the listed board games. For example, transform a program room into Candyland. Re-create Lollipop Woods, Gummy Hills, and the Gingerbread House using colorful foam squares as tiles, balloons, and decorations.

- *Gaming Fair:* Set up tables featuring games of different decades. Patrons are free to roam around and explore or sit down and play. This activity is a good addition to the Collector Con described in the "2000s" chapter, particularly if anyone participating in the Con is a board or video game collector.

- *Board Game 3-D Design:* Patrons can create their own 3-D pieces for a board game of their choice. Use a 3-D scanner or Xbox Kinect to scan patrons' heads or bodies and create personalized game pieces. Foam core boards can be used to create game boards, and patrons can make up their own rules.

CRATS

There are a lot of ways to repurpose old board games by crafting them into items that will get just as much use.

Bookmarks
- Using an X-acto knife or box cutter, cut 1½-by-6-inch pieces from a traditional game board. Using a hole punch, punch a hole in one end of each piece. Loop a piece of ribbon through the hole and voila! You have a bookmark.

Coasters
- Cut game boards into roughly 3-by-4-inch pieces and glue Scrabble tiles to them to make fun coasters. An option is to use pieces of cork in lieu of the game boards.

Ornaments
- Glue Scrabble tiles to tile holders from the game to spell out names or phrases. Attach screw eye hooks to either end and use a piece of ribbon to create a hanger. Patrons can make holiday ornaments or decorations to hang around the house.

Decoupage Notebook Covers
- Take the paper pieces from a board game (Monopoly money or cards from Clue, for example) and, using Mod Podge or decoupage glue, decorate the cover of a notebook.

MARKETING

Use board games to create your display! Include as many games as you can on the display with prompts such as, "Do you know when [board game] made its debut?" Include on the display, if possible, any books in your collection that have to do with the history of board games or even player guides.

VARIATIONS BY AGE GROUPS

Because this is intended to be an all-ages program (being mindful, of course, of age levels on certain games), the only variations necessary are those you choose from the given suggestions.

POPULAR FRANCHISES

Some franchises are so classic and iconic that they will never disappear completely from the pop culture stratosphere. You can't escape these franchises and shouldn't try because these franchises make the perfect pop cultural connections between generations and for all ages. They are consistently being revamped in different formats, keeping them fresh and new. Although many franchises are popular, Star Wars, Harry Potter, Jurassic Park, and Star Trek are just a few that are enduring and keep coming back! Celebrate each of these franchises with a festival or monthlong gala, and cap it off with a marathon session of the movies—just make sure your library has movie licenses before you show them.

PREP TIME	LENGTH OF PROGRAM	NUMBER OF PATRONS	SUGGESTED AGE RANGE
4–5 hours	3–4 hours (depending on number of activities and movies shown)	20–50	All ages

SUPPLIES/SHOPPING

3-D puzzles of choice

Readers' Theater Workshop and Green Screen
- Props
- Costumes
- Green screen

Bottle Cap Buttons
- Button maker (if available)
- Bottle caps
- Pin backings
- Resin
- Scissors
- Card stock

Bag Design
- Fabric bags
- Acrylic paint
- Paintbrushes
- Stencils or cutouts

Jurassic Park Dinosaur Eggs
- Model Magic
- Tools
- Plastic dinosaurs

Star Trek Communicator
- Card stock
- Pin backings
- Glue
- Scissors

Star Trek USS *Enterprise*
- Nuts
- Bolts
- Screws
- Washers
- Jewelry glue or Super Glue

Harry Potter Wands
- Decorative chopsticks
- Hot glue gun and glue sticks
- Tacky glue
- Liquid pens
- Puff paint
- Ribbons
- Glitter
- Embellishments

Star Wars Lightsabers
- Pool noodles
- Duct tape
- Sharpies or markers

ACTIVITIES AND CRAFTS

The following widely popular activities and crafts, which vary in cost and staff time, can be applied to all the franchises.

- *Fan Fiction Contest:* Host a fan fiction contest and collect entries over the course of a month. Add a twist to the program by asking contestants to include the library in their entry.

- *Readers' Theater Workshop and Green Screen:* Reenact favorite scenes in a Readers' Theater Workshop. Be sure to provide props and costumes for your patrons. If you want to challenge your staff and patrons, have them try to pare down one of the movies in the franchise into ninety seconds for fun and hilarious results. (This idea was inspired by James Kennedy's 90-Second Newbery contest.)

    Find or create iconic props from the movies (such as Harry Potter's glasses or a lightsaber) and make them available for pictures. If you have a green screen and can use a digital background, take advantage of this!

- *Bottle Cap Buttons:* Use bottle caps and resin, or a button maker if your library owns one, to create buttons for favorite quotes, icons, or characters from the franchise.

- *Bag Design:* Take a popular symbol from a beloved franchise and create cutouts for patrons to paint or silkscreen onto a fabric bag. You can also use popular quotes or a silhouette of an iconic character. *Examples:*

  » Jurassic Park: "Clever Girl" with a raptor
  » Star Wars: "Do or do not. There is no try" with the symbol of the Rebel Alliance
  » Star Trek: "Live long and prosper" with the Vulcan symbol
  » Harry Potter: "I solemnly swear that I am up to no good" with glasses and a lightning bolt

Jurassic Park

- *Dig!:* Create a dinosaur excavation site in your library. Bury dinosaur treasures, clues, and fossil re-creations. This is a great chance for patrons to get hands-on experience with a "dig site" and learn how to identify different bones of dinosaurs.

- Invite a paleontology student or professor to speak about her experience studying dinosaurs. Ask the speaker to bring in artifacts and fossils, if possible. This is a great opportunity for a museum or exhibit partnership with the library.

- *Jurassic Park Dinosaur Eggs:* Use Model Magic and plastic dinosaurs to create a dinosaur in an egg. Alternatively, create eggs ahead of time, hide the eggs around your library or children's section, and send patrons on a dinosaur hunt! When all the eggs have been found, extract the dinosaurs from the eggs using small tools.

Star Trek

- *Star Trek Communicator:* Create your own Combadge or Communicator. Use gold card stock to design the badge and, if needed, create templates for the two pieces to fit together. Glue and add the pin backing. If the badge doesn't pass the test, you're officially a Red Shirt!

- *Star Trek USS* Enterprise: Design a miniature magnet of the USS *Enterprise* out of nuts and bolts. Instructions can be found on the Instructables site (www .instructables.com/id/Easy-Handmade-Nuts-and-Bolts-Enterprise/).

Harry Potter

- *Harry Potter Wands:* Decorate your own wand with personality and pizzazz. Buy decorative chopsticks from a local craft store and let your patrons go wild. Use liquid pens, puff paint, ribbons, glitter, and other embellishments to make wands as unique as the wizards themselves. Adhere decor using a hot glue gun or tacky glue.

- *Harry Potter Yule Ball:* Hold a Yule Ball for your patrons and dance the night away! Deck the library with decorations, encourage patrons to dress in their best wizarding wear (or formal wear), serve butterbeer and Honeydukes treats, and rock out to your favorite wizard rock songs.

Star Wars

- *Star Wars Lightsabers:* Create lightsabers out of pool noodles with this cheap and fun DIY craft. All you need are pool noodles and duct tape or Sharpies or markers (find instructions on the Disney Family Newsletter website: https://family .disney.com/craft/how-to-make-a-star-wars-inspired-lightsaber-from-pool -noodles/). This craft can also lead to lightsaber duels, which you can choose to embrace as an activity, if desired.

- *Jedi Training Academy:* Send your patrons to the Jedi Training Academy. Task them with obstacle courses, exercise routines, lightsaber training, and, of course, Star Wars history and trivia. If they pass, be sure to give them a Jedi Knight Training Certificate.

TRIVIA AND OTHER FREE GAMES

All of these franchises have rabid fan bases who would appreciate a challenging game of trivia. One option is to form teams comprised of different generations (for example, Star Wars: Adults versus Teens, or Tween versus Teen: Harry Potter Smackdown). These popular franchises all have original sources: books. Use them as inspiration for your trivia questions and be open to the idea of a book trivia night or a book versus movie trivia program.

MARKETING

- Tie in your choice of the franchise with an already celebrated day in the franchise, such as July 31 for Harry Potter's birthday or May 4 (May the Fourth be with you) to celebrate Star Wars.

- *3-D Puzzles:* Encourage patrons to help assemble 3-D puzzles of icons or places for your advertised franchise, such as the Millennium Falcon or Hogwarts. Use this activity to generate excitement for the series and to advertise the events. You can also include it as part of an event.

PRO TIP

Many of these programs and activities can work as crossovers with "Reboot Month." Star Wars, Star Trek, Harry Potter, and Jurassic Park all have rebooted movies from their original series.

REBOOT MONTH

If the dawn of the new millennium proved anything, it's that pop culture is nothing if not cyclical. The 2010s have given us a plethora of reboots of popular television series and movie franchises, with more on the horizon. In this age of peak nostalgia, we propose planning an entire month of weekend reboot and remake viewings, with additional tie-in programming peppered in. Obviously the movies you choose to feature are up to you (and your library's movie licenses), but here are some examples.

PREP TIME	LENGTH OF PROGRAM	NUMBER OF PATRONS	SUGGESTED AGE RANGE
6–7 hours	2–2½ hours for each film viewing	Dependent on space for movie viewings	Dependent on movie

SUPPLIES/SHOPPING

- Projection screen
- Digital projector
- DVD player
- Snacks (see the activities section for suggestions)

ACTIVITIES

The schedule of viewings will best be determined by the movies you're showing and how you want to show them. For example, you might want to create a mini film fest in which patrons view both the original film and its reboot together. Alternatively, you might want to space the viewings out and show the original and the reboot on different days. Another option is MuViChat—viewers can interact with the films on their personal devices or on iPads that you provide to them. Whichever option you choose, be sure to provide movie snacks—and don't forget the popcorn!

Movies:
- *Ghostbusters* (1984) and *Ghostbusters* (2016) (Consider crossing over with the "Ghostbusted" program in the "1980s" section.)
  SNACK IDEAS: Ecto Coolers (see recipe in the "1980s" chapter), Slimer food (Cheerios, mini marshmallows, pretzels, licorice bites, M&M's)

- *TRON* (1982) and *TRON: Legacy* (2010)
  SNACK IDEA: Astronaut ice cream

- *Planet of the Apes* (1968) and *Planet of the Apes* (2001)
  SNACK IDEA: Banana fondue

- *Jurassic Park* (1993) and *Jurassic World* (2015)
  SNACK IDEA: Jell-O snack packs

CRAFTS

If you are targeting all ages with your mini fest, consider including simple crafts like coloring sheets that are related to the movies you are showing.

TRIVIA AND OTHER FREE GAMES

Although participants likely won't have time to play trivia during the movie fest, consider printing out sheets of information, including trivia, about each movie you're showing and making the sheets available to patrons. Or, if you are showing both movies on one day but have planned break time between each viewing (recommended), you can play a few rounds of trivia during that time.

MARKETING

Create a display of the movies that you'll be featuring for the month and include on it information about the series. Also include any additional materials (books, soundtracks, video games) related to the franchises that you'll be featuring.

VARIATIONS BY AGE GROUPS

Here are other title suggestions, including several that would work well for an all-ages audience.

- *Teenage Mutant Ninja Turtles* (1990) and *Teenage Mutant Ninja Turtles* (2014)

- *Star Trek* (1979) and *Star Trek* (2009)

- *Willy Wonka and the Chocolate Factory* (1971) and *Charlie and the Chocolate Factory* (2005)

- *Cinderella* (animated, 1950) and *Cinderella* (live-action, 2015)

- *Beauty and the Beast* (animated, 1991) and *Beauty and the Beast* (live-action, 2017)

TREATS AND BEATS BY THE DECADE

This is an easy and fun nostalgic trip to put together! Participants will enjoy hearing songs from different decades while having snacks.

PREP TIME	LENGTH OF PROGRAM	NUMBER OF PATRONS	SUGGESTED AGE RANGE
2 hours	1½ hours	35	Older adults, families

SUPPLIES/SHOPPING

- Snacks (see time line for possible selections; choose one from each decade)
- Plates
- Napkins

ACTIVITIES

- Offer a snack from each decade on the paper plates so audience members can pick them up as they arrive.

- Play one or two clips from popular songs from each decade beginning with patriotic wartime songs of the 1940s. Use music from the library's collection, either on CDs or downloaded from library sites like Freegal Music.

- See foodtimeline.org for snack ideas, but here are some possibilities:
  » **1940s:** Rice Krispies bars, M&M's
  » **1950s:** Chex Mix, thumbprint cookies
  » **1960s:** Pop Tarts, Pringles
  » **1970s:** Jelly Bellys, Pop Rocks
  » **1980s:** Jell-O Instant Pudding cups
  » **1990s:** Dirt cups, pretzel bread
  » **2000s:** Cake pops, cupcakes

MARKETING

- Make bookmarks listing the decades and popular music with information about the program.

- Display a time line with pictures or packages of popular snacks and foods. Pictures of popular bands would also be fun to see. Include information about the program.

VARIATIONS BY AGE GROUPS

Teens: Have teens guess the decade after hearing several different songs while sampling some of the snacks.

ABOUT THE AUTHORS

AMY J. ALESSIO is an award-winning librarian with a black belt in karate. Her latest coauthored reference title, *50+ Fandom Programs*, was published by ALA Editions in 2017. She teaches graduate level young adult literature and conducts dozens of webinars every year, including on the topic of social media for book lovers. She enjoys sharing her passion for Jell-O and kolackies with thirty local and national audiences a year during interactive presentations on vintage cookbooks and crafts. She reviews romance titles for *Booklist* and has authored and edited several works of fiction and nonfiction. She is a former board member for the Young Adult Library Services Association. Learn more at www.amyalessio.com.

KATIE LaMANTIA is a collection development-data management librarian at Baker and Taylor. She is a former teen advisory board member turned teen librarian and is the coauthor of the books, *50+ Fandom Programs* (ALA Editions, 2017) and *A Year of Programs for Millennials and More* (ALA Editions, 2015). She has a personal and professional appreciation and interest in pop culture and has presented at multiple state and national library conferences about pop culture, technology, and 20s and 30s programming. In her spare time she enjoys trivia, traveling, and extreme adventure activities.

EMILY VINCI is the fiction manager at the Schaumburg Township District Library in Schaumburg, Illinois. Her professional interests are promoting the acquisition and appreciation of comics and graphic novels in libraries as well as creating programming that targets patrons in their 20s and 30s. She presents frequently about pop culture and millennial-targeted programming and coauthored the books *A Year of Programs for Millennials and More* (ALA Editions, 2015) and *50+ Fandom Programs* (ALA Editions, 2017). A lifelong lover of all things pop culture and an avid collector, at the time of this writing Emily has more than two hundred copies of the Jurassic Park films on VHS and is always looking for more.

INDEX

A

A. V. Club, xiv
Academy of Model Aeronautics, 34
accessories
    Disney Accessories, 123, 124
    '80s Accessories, 54–56
action figures, '80s, 77, 78
activities
    for Attack of the Brat Pack, 57
    for Cake Pops, 98–99
    for Chex Mix and More: Nifty
        Fifties' Snacks, 3
    for Classic Candies by the Decade,
        118
    for Classic Cars, 120–121
    for Collector Con, 100
    for Cult Movie Fest, 102
    for Decades of Disney, 123
    for Decoupage Daydream, 20–21
    description of section, xvii
    for DIY Lava Lamps and Pet Rocks,
        42
    for Domino Day, 37
    for '80s Accessories, 55–56
    for Erector Set, Tinkertoy, and
        Lincoln Log Challenges, 39
    for Everything Barbie, 4
    for Fashion Trendsetters, 126–128
    for '50s Chic: Poodle Totes, 15–16
    for Flair Fun, 82–83
    for Flannel Pillows, 84–85
    for Games, 130
    for Ghostbusted, 60
    for Graffiti Art, 62–63
    for Holy Primetime, Batman!
        Superheroes on TV, 26
    for I Love Lucy, 6
    for I Want My MTV, 65–66
    for Love Beads, 28
    for Make Your Own BBQ, 12
    for Marvel Madness, 105
    for McDonald's Happy Meal Toys,
        43
    for Microwave Mania, 69
    for Model Train Mania, 14
    for The Name is Bond, James
        Bond program, 9
    for Nickelodeon Nostalgia Night,
        87–89

    for '90s Technology and Game
        Night, 80–81
    for Not Your Mother's Book Club:
        Books That Shocked, 30–31
    for 100 Years of Life: Board Game
        History and Challenges, 18–19
    for 100 Years of RC and Model
        Airplanes, 35
    for Pac-Man Party, 71–72
    for Pop Music: Boy Bands and Girl
        Power! 92
    for Popular Franchises, 133–135
    for Reality TV in Real Life, 108–109
    for Reboot Month, 136–137
    for Retro Crafts: Pom-Poms,
        Macramé, Flower Looms, and
        More, 46
    for Revenge of the Nerds, 111–112
    for Riot Grrrl Celebration: Zine
        and Button Making, 94
    for Rubik's Cube Challenge, 74
    for Tie-Dye, 48–49
    for Treats and Beats by the
        Decade, 138
    for TR-Not-So-L, 114
    for Y.A., Why Not? The Golden
        Age of Young Adult Literature,
        50–51
age groups
    See variations by age groups
airplanes, 34–35
*Amazing Fantastic Incredible: A
    Marvelous Memoir* (Lee & David), 105
Amazing Library Race program, 107,
    108, 109
The Amazing Race (television show),
    107
America's Got Talent night, 109
apparel
    See clothing
appliqué, 15–16
arcades, 70–73
Are You Afraid of the Dark? program,
    89, 90
Are You Afraid of the Dark? (television
    show), 87
art, Graffiti Art, 62–64
Attack of the Brat Pack, 57–58

B

bacon, 68, 69
Bag Design, 132, 134
bags
    denim bags/purses, 23, 24
    '50s Chic: Poodle Totes, 15–16
Baking Trivia game, 99
barbecue, 11–12
*Barbie and Ruth: The Story of the
    World's Most Famous Doll and the
    Woman Who Created Her* (Gerber), 4
barrettes, ribbon, 54, 55
Batman, 26–27
Beach Ball Boulders game, 109
beads
    Love Beads, 28–29
    in Marvel Madness, 104, 105
    Pac-Man Perler beads, 72
Beauty and the Beast (animated,
    1991), 137
Beauty and the Beast (live-action,
    2017), 137
best practices, xv–xvi
beverages
    See food/drinks
The Big Bang Theory (television show),
    110
BlueKatKraft blog, 128
Blume, Judy, 51
board games
    Board Game 3-D Design, 129, 130
    100 Years of Life: Board Game
        History and Challenges, 18–19
Bond, James, 8–10
book club, 30–31
book discussion
    on Batman '66/Wonder Woman
        '77, 27
    for Everything Barbie program, 4
    for Marvel Madness, 105
    for The Name is Bond, James Bond
        program, 8, 9
    for Revenge of the Nerds, 110,
        111–112
    Young at Heart Book Discussion
        Group, 51
bookmarks
    from board game, 129, 131

bookmarks (*continued*)
for Classic Candies by the Decade, 119
for Treats and Beats by the Decade, 139
books
best practices for pop culture programs, xvi
Disney Book to Movie, 123
Not Your Mother's Book Club: Books That Shocked, 30–31
trends in, xiv
Y.A., Why Not? The Golden Age of Young Adult Literature, 50–51
Bottle Cap Buttons, 132, 133
Boy Bands, 91–93
bracelets, denim, 25
Brat Pack Trivia, 58
Braver, Rita, 51
breakdancing, 66
building toys, 39–40
buttons
Bottle Cap Buttons, 132, 133
Marvel Madness, 104, 105
Riot Grrrl Celebration: Zine and Button Making, 94–95
BuzzFeed, xiv
BYOG (Bring Your Own Game), 125

C
Cabbage Patch Kids, 76–78
Cake Pops, 98–99
candy, Classic Candies by the Decade, 118–119
CandyFavorites.com, 118
Car Care 101, 121
Car Movie Fest, 121
Care Bears, 77
cars, Classic Cars, 120–121
Cars-by-the-Decade Photo Contest, 120
cassette tape pencil holder, 65, 66, 114, 115
CD coasters, 65, 66–67
CDs, 115
charades, 112
Charlie and the Chocolate Factory (2005), 137
Charlot, Juli Lynne, 15
checkers, 6, 7
cheese and salsa dip, 68, 69
Chex Mix and More: Nifty Fifties' Snacks, 2–3
Chocolate by the Decade, 119
chocolate tasting, 6–7
Cinderella (animated, 1950), 137
Cinderella (live-action, 2015), 137
circulation, xv
Classic Candies by the Decade, 118–119

Classic Cars, 120–121
Classic Pac-Man, 70, 71
clothing
Everything Denim, 23–25
Fashion Trendsetters, 126–128
Flair Fun, 82–83
Tie-Dye, 48–49
trends in, xiv
clues, 108
coasters
from board game, 131
CD coasters, 65, 66–67
Collector Con
crossover with Everything Barbie, 4
crossover with Marvel Madness, 105
Gaming Fair and, 130
instructions for, 100–101
collector fair, 77
comics
Collector Con, 101
Holy Primetime, Batman! Superheroes on TV, 27
Marvel Madness, 104–106
Revenge of the Nerds, 110, 112
communication, xvi
community partnerships, xvi
computer, Take-Apart Night, 81
costume contest, 57
Costume Sing-Along, 122, 123
crafts
for Attack of the Brat Pack, 58
board games, repurposing, 131
for Classic Cars, 121
for Decades of Disney, 124
Decoupage Daydream, 20–22
description of section, xvii
DIY Lava Lamps and Pet Rocks, 41–42
for Domino Day, 37
for Erector Set, Tinkertoy, and Lincoln Log Challenges, 39
for Everything Barbie, 5
for Everything Denim, 24–25
for Fashion Trendsetters, 128
'50s Chic: Poodle Totes, 15–16
Flair Fun, 82–83
Flannel Pillows program, 84–85
for Games, 131
for Ghostbusted, 60–61
for Graffiti Art, 63
for Holy Primetime, Batman! Superheroes on TV, 26–27
for I Love Lucy, 7
for I Want My MTV, 66–67
Love Beads, 28–29
for Marvel Madness, 105
McDonald's Happy Meal Toys, 43–44
for Nickelodeon Nostalgia Night, 89
for 100 Years of Life: Board Game History and Challenges, 19

for Pac-Man Party, 72
for Pop Music: Boy Bands and Girl Power! 92–93
for Popular Franchises, 133–135
for Reboot Month, 137
Retro Crafts: Pom-Poms, Macramé, Flower Looms, and More, 45–47
for Revenge of the Nerds, 112
Riot Grrrl Celebration: Zine and Button Making, 94–95
for Rubik's Cube Challenge, 75
Tie-Dye, 48–49
for TR-Not-So-L, 115
"Crafts of the '60s" (hubpages.com), 28–29
Crayon Tie-Dye, 49
Cult Movie Fest, 102–103
cultural sensitivity, xvi
cycle, of pop culture, xiii

D
dancing, 65–66
David, Peter, 105
DC Comics, 27
Decades of Disney, 122–125
Decoupage Daydream, 20–22
Decoupage Notebook Covers, 130, 131
denim
bags/purses, 23, 24
board, 23, 24
bracelets, 25
Everything Denim, 23–25
journal cover, 23, 24
detection devices, 60
Dig! activity, 134
dioramas, 122, 124
Disney, Decades of, 122–125
Disney Accessories, 123, 124
Disney Book to Movie, 122, 123
Disney Movie Roast, 122, 123
Disney Peep Art Dioramas, 122, 124
display
for Collector Con, 101
for Decades of Disney, 125
for Everything Barbie, 5
for games, 131
for I Love Lucy, 7
for The Name is Bond, James Bond program, 10
for Reality TV in Real Life, 109
for Reboot Month, 137
for Revenge of the Nerds, 112
for Treats and Beats by the Decade, 139
for TR-Not-So-L, 115
DIY Board Games, 19
DIY Disney Hacked Dresses, 122, 124
DIY Lava Lamps and Pet Rocks, 41–42
DIY TV trays, 26–27

dolls
    Everything Barbie, 4–5
    Strawberry Shortcake, Cabbage
        Patch Kids, and Other Hot '80s
        Toys, 76–78
Domino Brownies, 36, 37
Domino Day, 36–38
domino magnets, 36, 37
Double Dare program, 86, 88
dress, DIY Disney Hacked Dresses,
    122, 124
drinks
    See food/drinks
drones, 34–35
Duncan, Lois, 51

E

earrings, plastic geometric, 54, 55
Ecto Cooler, 59, 60
Edible Cars, 120, 121
Egg Walk, 113
'80s Accessories, 54–56
'80s Prom, 57
Elephant Toothpaste, 113
Empire Records (movie), 94
Entertainment Weekly, xiv
Erector Set, Tinkertoy, and Lincoln
    Log Challenges, 39–40
Escape Room, 8, 9
Estevz, Emilio, 57–58
Everything Barbie, 4–5
Everything Denim, 23–25
Exit Through the Gift Shop
    (documentary film), 63

F

families
    Cake Pops for, 99
    Flair Fun for, 83
    Flannel Pillows for, 85
    Nickelodeon Nostalgia Night for, 90
    100 Years of Life: Board Game
        History and Challenges for, 19
fan art contest, 113
Fan Fiction Contest, 133
Fan Fiction Mashup, 110, 111
fandom
    DIY Board Games, 19
    Revenge of the Nerds, 110–113
    trends, identifying, xiv
Fandom Perler beads, 111, 112
The Fangirl Life (Smith), 110
The Fangirl's Guide to the Galaxy
    (Maggs), 110
fashion
    DIY Disney Hacked Dresses, 124
    '80s Accessories, 54–56
    See also clothing
Fashion Trendsetters, 126–128

Fear Factor program, 107, 108, 109
Fear Factor (television show), 107
felting, 15–16
'50s Chic: Poodle Totes, 15–16
Fisher-Price Little People, 77, 78
Flair Fun, 82–83
Flannel Pillows, 84–85
Flashdance (movie), 56
Fleming, Ian, 8
flower looms, 45–47
Flowerpot Hibachi, 11, 12
food/drinks
    Cake Pops, 98–99
    Chex Mix and More: Nifty Fifties'
        Snacks, 2–3
    chocolate tasting for I Love Lucy
        program, 6
    Classic Candies by the Decade,
        118–119
    Domino Brownies, 36
    for Fear Factor, 108
    list of ingredients for, xvi
    Make Your Own BBQ, 11–12
    Martini Mixology, 8, 9
    Microwave Mania, 68–69
    for Revenge of the Nerds, 110,
        113
    Strawberry Shortcake, 76
    Treats and Beats by the Decade,
        138–139
*Forever Barbie: The Unauthorized
    Biography of a Real Doll* (Lord), 4
fortune telling, 38
fossils, 134
Franchises, Popular, 132–135
Freaks and Geeks (television show),
    113
freestyle graffiti session, 63
French toast, 68, 69

G

games
    Domino Day, 36–38
    Games program, 129–131
    '90s Technology and Game Night,
        80–81
    See also trivia/other free games
Games by the Decade, 130
Gaming Fair, 130
Garbage Pail Kids, 77
geek, 110
Geek Out, 111
Gerber, R., 4
Ghostbusted, 59–61
Ghostbusters (1984), 59, 61, 136
Ghostbusters (2016), 59, 61, 136
Ghostbusters: Chicago Division
    recipe, 60
Girl Bands, 91–93
Girl Power program, 92–93

girls, Riot Grrrl Celebration: Zine and
    Button Making, 94–95
gloves, fingerless, 54, 55
Gone Fishing game, 108
*The Good, the Bad, and the Barbie: A
    Doll's History and Her Impact on Us*
    (Stone), 4
Google Analytics, xiii
Graffiti Art, 62–64
Green, John and Hank, 111
Guess the Superhero game, 27

H

hair, 6, 91, 92
Hall, Anthony Michael, 57–58
Happy Meal Toys, 43–44
Harry Potter
    nerds in pop culture, 110
    Popular Franchises, 132–135
Harry Potter Wands, 133, 134
Harry Potter Yule Ball, 135
headbands, 54, 55, 124
headings, of programs, xvi–xvii
He-Man, 77
Hinton, S. E., 50
Holiday Candies by the Decade, 119
Holy Primetime, Batman! Superheroes
    on TV, 26–27
Hot Wheels Track Racing, 120, 121
Howe, Sean, 105
Hughes, John, 57–58

I

I Love Lucy, 6–7
I Want My MTV
    crossover with Attack of the Brat
        Pack program, 57
    crossover with Pop Music: Boy
        Bands and Girl Power! 93
    instructions for, 65–67
Injured Teammate Mummy Wrap
    game, 108

J

James Bond program, 8–10
jeans, 23–25
Jedi Training Academy, 135
Jem, 77
jewelry
    See accessories
Jurassic Park (1993), 137
Jurassic Park Dinosaur Eggs, 132,
    134
Jurassic Park, Popular Franchises
    program, 132–135
Jurassic World (2015), 137

K

karaoke
    for Pop Music: Boy Bands and Girl
        Power! 91, 92
    for TR-Not-So-L, 114–115
karate, 10
Keep Talking and Nobody Explodes,
    8, 9

L

lava lamp
    DIY Lava Lamps and Pet Rocks,
        41–42
    Lava Lamp Science, 113
Lee, Stan, 105
leg warmers, 54, 55
Legends of the Hidden Temple
    (television show), 86, 87–88
length of program, xvii
library staff, xvi
Life board game, 18–19
Life flash fiction, 19
Life Tile/People keychains, 18, 19
Life-Size Gaming, 129, 130
Live Pac-Man, 70, 71–72
lollipop, 98–99
Lord, M. G., 4
Lord of the Rings (movies), 110
Love Beads, 28–29
Lowe, Rob, 57–58
lyrics.com, 115

M

macramé
    Retro Crafts: Pom-Poms, Macramé,
        Flower Looms, and More, 45–47
    updating for programs today, xv
Maggs, Sam, 110
Make Your Own BBQ, 11–12
makeup and hair tutorial, 6
marketing
    for Attack of the Brat Pack, 58
    for Cake Pops, 99
    for Chex Mix and More: Nifty
        Fifties' Snacks, 3
    for Classic Candies by the Decade,
        119
    for Classic Cars, 121
    for Collector Con, 101
    for Cult Movie Fest, 103
    for Decades of Disney, 125
    for Decoupage Daydream, 22
    description of section, xvii
    DIY Lava Lamps and Pet Rocks, 42
    for Domino Day, 38
    for '80s Accessories, 56
    for Erector Set, Tinkertoy, and
        Lincoln Log Challenges, 39
    for Everything Barbie, 5
    for Everything Denim, 25
    for Fashion Trendsetters, 128
    for '50s Chic: Poodle Totes, 16
    for Flair Fun, 83
    for Flannel Pillows, 85
    for Games, 131
    for Ghostbusted, 61
    for Graffiti Art, 63
    for Holy Primetime, Batman!
        Superheroes on TV, 27
    for I Love Lucy, 7
    for I Want My MTV, 67
    for Love Beads, 29
    for Make Your Own BBQ, 12
    for Marvel Madness, 106
    for McDonald's Happy Meal Toys,
        44
    for Microwave Mania, 69
    for Model Train Mania, 14
    for The Name is Bond, James
        Bond program, 10
    for Nickelodeon Nostalgia Night, 90
    for '90s Technology and Game
        Night, 81
    for Not Your Mother's Book Club:
        Books That Shocked, 31
    for 100 Years of RC and Model
        Airplanes, 35
    for 100 Years of Life: Board Game
        History and Challenges, 19
    for Pac-Man Party, 73
    for Pop Music: Boy Bands and Girl
        Power! 93
    for Popular Franchises, 135
    for Reality TV in Real Life, 109
    for Reboot Month, 137
    for Retro Crafts: Pom-Poms,
        Macramé, Flower Looms, and
        More, 47
    for Revenge of the Nerds, 112
    for Riot Grrrl Celebration: Zine
        and Button Making, 95
    for Rubik's Cube Challenge, 75
    for Tie-Dye, 49
    for Treats and Beats by the
        Decade, 139
    for TR-Not-So-L, 115
    for Y.A., Why Not? The Golden Age
        of Young Adult Literature, 51
Marshmallow Man, 61
Marshmallow Structures, 59, 61
Martini Mixology, 8, 9
Marvel Comics: The Untold Story
    (Howe), 105
Marvel Madness, 104–106
mason jars, 20, 21
McCarthy, Andrew, 57–58
McDonald's Happy Meal Toys, 43–44
Mickey or Minnie Mouse Headband,
    124
Microwave Mania, 68–69

A Mighty Girl (blog), 51
millennials
    Domino Brownies for, 38
    '80s Accessories for, 56
    Everything Denim for, 25
    '50s Chic: Poodle Totes for, 16
    Flannel Pillows for, 85
    Ghostbusted for, 61
    Holy Primetime, Batman!
        Superheroes on TV for, 27
    Marvel Madness for, 106
    Microwave Mania, movie to go
        with, 69
    Nickelodeon Nostalgia Night for,
        86–90
    Reality TV in Real Life for, 109
    Revenge of the Nerds for, 113
Mini Planter Tabletop Grill, 11, 12
Minute to Win It games, 108–109
model airplanes, 34–35
Model Train Mania, 13–14
Moore, Demi, 57–58
movie release dates, xiii
movie screenings, 57
movies
    Attack of the Brat Pack, 57–58
    best practices for pop culture
        programs, xv, xvi
    Car Movie Fest, 121
    Cult Movie Fest, 102–103
    Disney Book to Movie, 123
    Disney Movie Roast, 123
    for '80s Accessories program, 56
    Marvel Madness, 104–106
    The Name is Bond, James Bond
        program, 8–10
    Reboot Month, 136–137
    for Riot Grrrl Celebration: Zine
        and Button Making, 94
    Y.A., Why Not? The Golden Age of
        Young Adult Literature, 50–51
MTV
    I Want My MTV, 57, 65–67, 93
    TR-Not-So-L, 114–115
mural, 63, 64
music
    I Want My MTV, 65–67
    Pop Music: Boy Bands and Girl
        Power! 91–93
    Treats and Beats by the Decade,
        138–139
    TR-Not-So-L, 114–115
Music Video Remake, 91, 92
MuViChat, 136
Myers, Walter Dean, 51

N

The Name is Bond, James Bond
    program, 8–10
National Railroad Association, 13

National Toy Train Museum, 13
necklace
    Pendant Necklaces, 126, 128
    Ursula Seashell Necklace, 124
Nelson, Judd, 57–58
Nerd Snacks, 110, 111
Nerd Tote Bag, 111, 112
Nerdfighters, 110, 111
nerds, Revenge of the Nerds, 110–113
Nickelodeon Nostalgia Night, 86–90
1980s programs
    Attack of the Brat Pack, 57–58
    '80s Accessories, 54–56
    Fashion Trendsetters activities
        for, 127
    Ghostbusted, 59–61
    Graffiti Art, 62–64
    I Want My MTV, 65–67
    Microwave Mania, 68–69
    overview of, 53
    Pac-Man Party, 70–73
    Rubik's Cube Challenge, 74–75
    Strawberry Shortcake, Cabbage
        Patch Kids, and Other Hot '80s
        Toys, 76–78
    trends from 1980s, xiii
    trends that will work for programs
        today, xv
1950s programs
    Chex Mix and More: Nifty Fifties'
        Snacks, 2–3
    Everything Barbie, 4–5
    Fashion Trendsetters activities
        for, 126
    '50s Chic: Poodle Totes, 15–16
    I Love Lucy, 6–7
    Make Your Own BBQ, 11–12
    Model Train Mania, 13–14
    The Name is Bond, James Bond,
        8–10
    overview of, 1
1990s programs
    Fashion Trendsetters activities
        for, 127
    Flair Fun, 82–83
    Flannel Pillows, 84–85
    Nickelodeon Nostalgia Night,
        86–90
    '90s Technology and Game Night,
        80–81
    overview of, 79
    Pop Music: Boy Bands and Girl
        Power! 91–93
    Riot Grrrl Celebration: Zine and
        Button Making, 94–95
1970s programs
    100 Years of RC and Model
        Airplanes, 34–35
    DIY Lava Lamps and Pet Rocks,
        41–42
    Domino Day, 36–38

Erector Set, Tinkertoy, and Lincoln
    Log Challenges, 39–40
Fashion Trendsetters activities
    for, 127
McDonald's Happy Meal Toys,
    43–44
overview of, 33
Retro Crafts: Pom-Poms, Macramé,
    Flower Looms, and More, 45–47
Tie-Dye, 48–49
Y.A., Why Not? The Golden Age of
    Young Adult Literature, 50–51
1960s programs
    Decoupage Daydream, 20–22
    Everything Denim, 23–25
    Fashion Trendsetters activities for,
        126–127
    Holy Primetime, Batman!
        Superheroes on TV, 26–27
    Love Beads, 28–29
    Not Your Mother's Book Club:
        Books That Shocked, 30–31
    100 Years of Life: Board Game
        History and Challenges, 18–19
    overview of, 17
'90s Game Night, 80, 81
'90s Hair, 91, 92
'90s Tech ID, 80
'90s Technology and Game Night,
    80–81
nostalgia
    never goes out of style, xiii
    Nickelodeon Nostalgia Night,
        86–90
    power of for library program, xvi
    Reboot Month, 136–137
Not Your Mother's Book Club: Books
    That Shocked, 30–31
Now That's What I Call Music!
    (compilation album), 115
number of patrons section, xvii

O
Office Space (movie), 82, 83
older adults
    Cake Pops for, 99
    Domino Brownies for, 38
    '80s Accessories for, 56
    Everything Denim for, 25
    Ghostbusted for, 61
    Marvel Madness for, 106
    '90s Technology and Game Night
        for, 81
    100 Years of Life: Board Game
        History and Challenges for, 19
    Pop Music: Boy Bands and Girl
        Power! for, 93
    Reality TV in Real Life for, 109
    Young at Heart Book Discussion
        Group, 51

100 Years of Life: Board Game
    History and Challenges, 18–19
100 Years of RC and Model Airplanes,
    34–35
origami
    Everything Barbie, 4–5
    I Love Lucy, 6–7
ornaments, 129, 131
The Outsiders (Hinton), 50

P
Pac-Man Party, 58, 70–73
Pac-Man Perler beads, 72
Pac-Man Picture Frames, 70, 72
patrons, xv
pencil holder, cassette tape, 65, 66,
    114, 115
pencils, Decoupage Daydream, 20, 21
Pendant Necklaces, 126, 128
Perler beads, 72, 104, 105
Pet Rocks, 41–42
photo cubes, 75
photos
    drone photo contest, 35
    for Fashion Trendsetters, 126–128
pillows, Flannel Pillows program,
    84–85
Planet of the Apes (1968), 137
Planet of the Apes (2001), 137
pom-poms, 45–47
poodle totes, 15–16
pop culture, xiii
pop culture programs
    best practices, xv–xvi
    ideas for/headings of, xvi–xvii
    past trends that will work for
        programs today, xiv–xv
    trends, identifying, xiii–xiv
pop culture review programs
    Classic Candies by the Decade,
        118–119
    Classic Cars, 120–121
    Decades of Disney, 122–125
    Fashion Trendsetters, 126–128
    Games, 129–131
    overview of, 117
    Popular Franchises, 132–135
    Reboot Month, 136–137
    Treats and Beats by the Decade,
        138–139
Pop Music: Boy Bands and Girl
    Power! 91–93
popcorn, microwave, 68, 69
Popular Franchises, 132–135
posters, 93, 109
prep time, xvii
presenter, 4
pro tips
    for Cake Pops, 99
    for Decades of Disney, 125

pro tips (*continued*)
 description of section, xvii
 for Erector Set, Tinkertoy, and
  Lincoln Log Challenges, 39
 for Everything Denim, 25
 for Fashion Trendsetters, 128
 for Ghostbusted, 61
 for Graffiti Art, 64
 for Marvel Universe, 106
 for Microwave Mania, 69
 for The Name is Bond, James
  Bond program, 10
 for '90s Technology and Game
  Night, 81
 for Pac-Man Party, 73
 for Pop Music: Boy Bands and Girl
  Power! 93
 for Popular Franchises, 135
 for Reality TV in Real Life, 109
 for Tie-Dye, 49
 for TR-Not-So-L, 115
"Protecting 'The Books That Will
 Never Be Written': Judy Blume's
 Fight Against Censorship" (*A Mighty
 Girl* blog), 51
punk movement, 94–95

R

radio control (RC), 34–35
Rainbow Brite Coloring Station, 76,
 77
Rainworks, 63
R/C Airplane World website, 34
RC model airplanes, 34–35
Readers' Theater Workshop and
 Green Screen, 132, 133
Real Genius (movie), 69
Reality Bites (movie), 94
Reality TV in Real Life, 107–109
Reboot Month
 crossover with Decades of Disney,
  125
 crossover with Popular Franchises,
  135
 instructions for, 136–137
remote control cars, track for, 121
resources
 for Fashion Trendsetters, 126–128
 for identifying trends, xiv
Retro Crafts: Pom-Poms, Macramé,
 Flower Looms, and More, 45–47
Revenge of the Nerds, 110–113
riddles, 108
Ringwald, Molly, 57–58
Riot Grrrl Celebration: Zine and
 Button Making, 93, 94–95
Rubik, Erno, 74
Rubik's Cube Challenge, 74–75
Rubik's Cubes, 77
Ruwix (Rubik's Cube wiki), 74

S

Salute Your Shorts summer camp
 session, 89
Salute Your Shorts (television show), 87
scavenger hunt, 10
School Spirit game, 99
Scrabble tiles, 131
scrunchies
 in Attack of the Brat Pack program, 58
 '80s Accessories, 55, 56
 flannel, 85
Sharpie Tie-Dye T-Shirt, 48, 49
Sheedy, Ally, 57–58
She-Ra, 77
shoe flair, 83
Shrine of the Silver Monkey, 87–88
sidewalk chalk art, 64
singing
 Costume Sing-Along, 123
 Pop Music: Boy Bands and Girl
  Power! 91, 92
 TR-Not-So-L, 114–115
slime, 59, 60, 90
Slimer, 61
Smith, Kathleen, 110
snacks
 Chex Mix and More: Nifty Fifties'
  Snacks, 2–3
 for Reboot Month, 136–137
 Treats and Beats by the Decade,
  138–139
 See also food/drinks
Snow White Apple, 124
solitaire, 37
Soup Can Succulent Holders, 20, 21
spy program, 8–10
Star Trek (1979), 137
Star Trek (2009), 137
Star Trek Communicator, 133, 134
Star Trek, Popular Franchises
 program, 132–135
Star Trek USS *Enterprise*, 133, 134
Star Wars Lightsabers, 133, 135
Star Wars, Popular Franchises
 program, 132–135
stereotypes, xvi
Stone, T. L., 4
stories, 111
storyteller, 60
Stouffer's Frozen French Bread Pizza,
 68, 69
Stranger Things (television show), xv
Strawberry Shortcake, Cabbage Patch
 Kids, and Other Hot '80s Toys, 76–78
Style Wars (documentary film), 63
suggested age range, xvii
Super Bowl season, 2–3
superheroes
 Holy Primetime, Batman!
  Superheroes on TV, 26–27
 Marvel Madness, 104–106

supplies/shopping
 for Attack of the Brat Pack, 57
 for Cake Pops, 98
 for Chex Mix and More: Nifty
  Fifties' Snacks, 2–3
 for Classic Candies by the Decade,
  118
 for Classic Cars, 120
 for Collector Con, 100
 for Cult Movie Fest, 102
 for Decades of Disney, 122–123
 Decoupage Daydream, 20
 description of section, xvii
 DIY Lava Lamps and Pet Rocks, 41
 for Domino Day, 36
 for '80s Accessories, 54–55
 for Erector Set, Tinkertoy, and
  Lincoln Log Challenges, 39
 for Everything Barbie, 4
 for Everything Denim, 23–24
 for Fashion Trendsetters, 126
 for '50s Chic: Poodle Totes, 15
 for Flair Fun, 82
 for Flannel Pillows, 84
 for Games, 129–130
 for Ghostbusted, 59
 for Graffiti Art, 62
 for Holy Primetime, Batman!
  Superheroes on TV, 26
 for I Love Lucy, 6
 for I Want My MTV, 65
 for Love Beads, 28
 for Make Your Own BBQ, 11
 for Marvel Madness, 104
 for McDonald's Happy Meal Toys,
  43
 for Microwave Mania, 68
 for Model Train Mania, 13
 for The Name is Bond, James
  Bond program, 8
 for Nickelodeon Nostalgia Night,
  86–87
 for Not Your Mother's Book Club:
  Books That Shocked, 30
 for 100 Years of Life: Board Game
  History and Challenges, 18
 for 100 Years of RC and Model
  Airplanes, 34
 for Pac-Man Party, 70
 for Pop Music: Boy Bands and Girl
  Power! 91–92
 for Popular Franchises, 132–133
 for Reality TV in Real Life, 107
 for Reboot Month, 136
 for Retro Crafts: Pom-Poms,
  Macramé, Flower Looms, and
  More, 45–46
 for Revenge of the Nerds, 110–111
 for Riot Grrrl Celebration: Zine
  and Button Making, 94
 for Rubik's Cube Challenge, 74

for Tie-Dye, 48
for Treats and Beats by the
    Decade, 138
for TR-Not-So-L, 114
for Y.A., Why Not? The Golden Age
    of Young Adult Literature, 50
Survivor (television show), 107
Survivor program, 107, 108–109

T

Take-Apart Night, 80, 81
technology, '90s Technology and
    Game Night, 80–81
Teenage Mutant Ninja Turtles (1990),
    137
Teenage Mutant Ninja Turtles (2014),
    137
teens
    Everything Barbie for, 5
    Ghostbusted for, 61
    Holy Primetime, Batman!
        Superheroes on TV for, 27
    I Love Lucy for, 7
    Make Your Own BBQ for, 12
    Marvel Madness for, 106
    The Name is Bond, James Bond
        for, 10
    '90s Technology and Game Night
        for, 81
    Y.A., Why Not? The Golden Age of
        Young Adult Literature, 51
television
    Holy Primetime, Batman!
        Superheroes on TV, 26–27
    I Want My MTV, 65–67
    Nickelodeon Nostalgia Night, 86–90
    Reality TV in Real Life, 107–109
Temple Games, 88
Tesla, Nikola, 34
3-D puzzles, 135
Thriller Dance-Off activity, 65
Tie-Dye program, 48–49
time, xvi
Tin Can Grill, 11, 12
toothpaste, 113
toppling competition, 37
Total Request Live (TRL), 114–115
tournaments, 37
Toy Car Collecting, 121
toys
    Erector Set, Tinkertoy, and Lincoln
        Log Challenges, 39–40
    McDonald's Happy Meal Toys,
        43–44
    Model Train Mania, 13–14
    Rubik's Cube Challenge, 74–75
    Strawberry Shortcake, Cabbage
        Patch Kids, and Other Hot '80s
        Toys, 76–78
trains, Model Train Mania, 13–14

Treats and Beats by the Decade,
    138–139
trends
    cycle of, xiii
    Fashion Trendsetters, 126–128
    learning about, xiii–xiv
    past trends that will work for
        programs today, xiv–xv
trivia/other free games
    for Attack of the Brat Pack, 58
    for Cake Pops, 99
    for Classic Candies by the Decade,
        119
    for Cult Movie Fest, 103
    for Decades of Disney, 125
    description of section, xvii
    Double Dare, 88
    for Everything Barbie, 5
    for Fashion Trendsetters, 128
    for Ghostbusted, 61
    for Holy Primetime, Batman!
        Superheroes on TV, 27
    for I Love Lucy, 7
    for I Want My MTV, 67
    for Make Your Own BBQ, 12
    for Marvel Madness, 106
    for McDonald's Happy Meal Toys,
        44
    for Microwave Mania, 69
    for The Name is Bond, James
        Bond program, 9
    for Nickelodeon Nostalgia Night,
        89
    for '90s Technology and Game
        Night, 81
    for 100 Years of Life: Board Game
        History and Challenges, 19
    for Pac-Man Party, 72
    for Pop Music: Boy Bands and Girl
        Power! 93
    for Popular Franchises, 135
    for Reboot Month, 137
    for Revenge of the Nerds, 112
    for Riot Grrrl Celebration: Zine
        and Button Making, 95
    for Rubik's Cube Challenge, 75
    for TR-Not-So-L, 115
TR-Not-So-L program, 66, 114–115
TRON (1982), 137
TRON: Legacy (2010), 137
t-shirts
    '80s t-shirts, 55, 56
    for Flair Fun, 82–83
    Sharpie Tie-Dye T-Shirt, 48, 49
Tumblr, xiv
tutus, 55
TV trays, DIY, 26–27
tweens
    Domino Brownies for, 38
    Everything Barbie for, 5
    '50s Chic: Poodle Totes for, 16

Holy Primetime, Batman!
    Superheroes on TV for, 27
I Love Lucy for, 7
Marvel Madness for, 106
The Name is Bond, James Bond
    for, 10
Nickelodeon Nostalgia Night for,
    90
'90s Technology and Game Night
    for, 81
100 Years of RC and Model
    Airplanes for, 35
Pop Music: Boy Bands and Girl
    Power! for, 93
Revenge of the Nerds for, 113
Twitter, xiii
2000s programs
    Cake Pops, 98–99
    Collector Con, 100–101
    Cult Movie Fest, 102–103
    Fashion Trendsetters activities for,
        127–128
    Marvel Madness, 104–106
    overview of, 97
    Reality TV in Real Life, 107–109
    Revenge of the Nerds, 110–113
    TR-Not-So-L, 114–115

U

Upcycle That, 115
upcycling
    Decoupage Daydream, 20–22
    with Everything Denim, 23–25
Ursula Seashell Necklace, 124

V

variations by age groups
    for Attack of the Brat Pack, 58
    for Cake Pops, 99
    for Chex Mix and More: Nifty
        Fifties' Snacks, 3
    for Classic Candies by the Decade,
        119
    for Classic Cars, 121
    for Decades of Disney, 125
    for Decoupage Daydream, 22
    description of section, xvii
    DIY Lava Lamps and Pet Rocks, 42
    for Domino Day, 38
    for '80s Accessories, 56
    for Erector Set, Tinkertoy, and
        Lincoln Log Challenges, 39
    for Everything Barbie, 5
    for Everything Denim, 25
    for '50s Chic: Poodle Totes, 16
    for Flair Fun, 83
    for Flannel Pillows, 85
    for Games, 131
    for Ghostbusted, 61

variations by age groups (*continued*)
    for Graffiti Art, 64
    for Holy Primetime, Batman!
      Superheroes on TV, 27
    for I Love Lucy, 7
    for I Want My MTV, 67
    for Make Your Own BBQ, 12
    for Marvel Madness, 106
    for Microwave Mania, 69
    for Model Train Mania, 14
    for The Name is Bond, James
      Bond, 10
    for Nickelodeon Nostalgia Night, 90
    for '90s Technology and Game
      Night, 81
    for 100 Years of Life: Board Game
      History and Challenges, 19
    for 100 Years of RC and Model
      Airplanes, 35
    for Pop Music: Boy Bands and Girl
      Power! 93
    for Reality TV in Real Life, 109
    for Reboot Month, 137
    for Retro Crafts: Pom-Poms,
      Macramé, Flower Looms, and
      More, 47
    for Revenge of the Nerds, 113
    for Riot Grrrl Celebration: Zine
      and Button Making, 95
    for Rubik's Cube Challenge, 75
    for Tie-Dye, 49
    for Treats and Beats by the
      Decade, 139
    for TR-Not-So-L, 115
    for Y.A., Why Not? The Golden
      Age of Young Adult Literature,
      51
vest, 82–83
Vintage Car Show, 120

W
Walt Disney, 122–125
Water Challenge game, 109
We Need Diverse Books movement,
  51
website, 126–128
Wild Style (film), 63
Willy Wonka and the Chocolate Factory
  (movie), 137
writing, 111

Y
Y.A., Why Not? The Golden Age of
  Young Adult Literature, 50–51
young adult literature, 50–51
Young at Heart Book Discussion
  Group, 51
YouTube
    movies for YA literature program,
      50–51
    Nerdfighters channel, 111

Z
zine
    Marvel Madness, 104, 105
    Riot Grrrl Celebration: Zine and
      Button Making, 94–95